Emma

COLIN SIMPSON

EMMA

The Life of Lady Hamilton

THE BODLEY HEAD
LONDON SYDNEY
TORONTO

British Library Cataloguing
in Publication Data
Simpson, Colin
Emma, Lady Hamilton
I. Title
941.07′3′0924   DA483.H3
ISBN 0-370-30984-7

© Colin Simpson 1983
Printed in Great Britain for
The Bodley Head Ltd
9 Bow Street, London WC2E 7AL
by Redwood Burn Ltd, Trowbridge
First published 1983

CONTENTS

Acknowledgments

My principal debt is to Sir Harold Acton who steered me toward the archive material of the Bourbons of Naples, much of which is summarised in his own book of that name (London 1956). This rewarding study with its brilliant but friendly scholarship has been the catalyst of this book. A lesser but significant debt is due to the following Italian sources: Umberto Caldora's edition of the Diaries of Ferdinand IV 1796–1799 published in Naples 1965; Benedetto Croce's *La Rivoluzione Napoletana del 1799* (Bari 1912); *The Memoirs of General Pepe* (Lugano 1847); General Pietro Colletta's *History of the Kingdom of Naples 1734–1825* (Trans S. Horner, Edinburgh 1858); and *Naples in 1799* by Constance Giglioli (London 1903). Ms Carola Oman, whose definitive biography of *Nelson* (London 1947) still ranks above all others, drew attention to Sir John Laughton's essay on the bibliography of her subject—'It is enormous, but comparatively little of it has any real value'—and went on to analyse the legions of writers who have been drawn to the subject. I have unashamedly followed her judgments in my reading for I cannot see that they can be improved upon. Later books which I have found particularly helpful, and which were not available to Ms Oman, include Oliver Warner's *Emma Hamilton and Sir William* (London 1960), Brian Fothergill's *Sir William Hamilton* (London 1969), and Jack Russell's *Nelson and the Hamiltons* (London 1969), which introduced me to several new sources which he had discovered. Equally valuable has been H. C. Gutteridge's *Nelson and the Neapolitan Jacobins*, published by the Navy Records Society (Vol. XXV, London 1903).

However, the most valuable materials of all have been the letters, reports and private papers of many of the characters of this story. I am grateful to the trustees of the following institutions for allowing me unconditional access to their archives and permission to publish extracts:

    Cambridge: Fitzwilliam-Percival Bequest
    Edinburgh: National Library of Scotland MSS 3942
    Merton and Morden Public Library (Details of Merton Place)
    The Burney Collection of Newspapers 1800–1805

National Maritime Museum—Manuscript Collections
Phillips-Croker Collection
Phillips Collection
Bridport Collection
Matcham Collection
Nelson Ward Collection
Trafalgar House Collection
Girdlestone Collection
De Coppet Collection
Stewart Collection
Walter Collection
Montserrat Collection
Correspondence of Lady Nelson and James Warren
Transcript of the Monmouth Collection of Nelson Papers
Nelson Papers BGY/50
Nelson Papers-general
Correspondence of Lady Hamilton and Charles Greville
Correspondence of Lady Hamilton and Alexander Davison
    LBK/7
Correspondence of Lady Hamilton and George Rose
    LBK/50
Correspondence of Sir William Hamilton and Sir John
    Acton HML/21
Correspondence of Lady Nelson and Lord Hood HOO/28
Hugh Elliot Papers ELL/306
The Jervis Papers
The Keith Papers
The Sir John Orde Papers
Minto-Nelson-Hamilton Papers
The papers of Sir Edward Berry, Lord Collinwood, Sir
    John Duckworth and Alexander Scott
The Journal of HMS *Thalia* JOD/11
Lady Hamilton's songbook
Selected letters from Autograph collections Nos AGC/3/5/
    9/13/14/17/18/24/32
PST/10/39
FAC/1/2

British Museum—Manuscript Collections

ADD. MSS. 29914–5	Letters to Sir John Jervis
28333	Letters to Lady Nelson
30182	Letters of Captain W. Bedford
30260	Order book of HMS *Vanguard*
34048	Sir W. Hamilton to Sir J. Banks
34274	(G/f61) Nelson to Lady Hamilton
34710	Hamilton Papers
34902–88	Bridport Collection
37077	Letters of Sir W. Hamilton
40714–6	Hamilton and Greville Papers
41200	Letters to Sir W. Hamilton
38398–400	The Paget Papers
52360	Horatio Nelson's Commonplace book
1614	Nelson to Lady Hamilton
1617–20	Queen of Naples to Lady Hamilton
1623	Letters to Lord Nelson
2641	Sir John Banks to Sir William Hamilton

Finally my special thanks are due to those who have borne with me since the conception of this project in 1971: my wife, Jane, for her research and for her patience; Renata Riccasoli, for her skilful translations from often difficult 18th-century documents in Naples; and Ann Rye, an ideal secretary.

I

1765–1783

The Mistress
of Paddington Green

'. . . my virtue was vanquished,
but my sense of virtue was not overcome.'
Emma to the painter George Romney

The cold weather of January 1765 took a terrible toll
among the villages of the Wirral Peninsula in Cheshire. Up
in the hills, the bells of Great Neston Parish Church
cracked in the frost, and on the shore below the sea froze
along the sands of Dee. The port of Parkgate, then a
flourishing terminal for the Irish trade, was ice-bound and
the road that reached from the port, up and over the hills
and into the rich interior of Lancashire, was reduced to an
icy and deeply-rutted track, winding between great drifts
of frozen snow.

Towards the end of the month, a lone horseman rode
down to Parkgate. His name was George Henry Lyons: a
widower of sixty-five, a gentleman and land-owner by
birth, an amateur botanist by inclination; and, it is
reasonable to surmise, a cold, lonely and unhappy man.
His journey was to see his lawyer, his purpose, to
disinherit his only son Henry Lyons, then a consumptive
youth of eighteen. The father owned several hundred acres
at Den Hall which in those days was a substantial estate of
seven tenanted farms and most of the village of Great
Neston. However, his wife had died when his son Henry
was eleven years old, and he appeared to take very little

9

interest in either his house or his child. Instead he concentrated his energies on producing a privately-circulated bulletin which described the flora and fauna of the Wirral Peninsula. George Henry Lyons was more addicted to Latin tags than to the humanities, and to care for his son and his household he employed from the nearby village a widow called Mrs Kidd. Mrs Kidd, an accomplished seamstress and an excellent cook, brought with her her daughter, Mary, who was the same age as Henry. At first the two children saw little of each other, as Henry was attending Eton College at Windsor, but the damp air of the Thames bit deeply into his lungs, and in 1763 when he was just sixteen he returned home to continue his studies under a tutor. Henry apparently also received a degree of tutelage from Mary Kidd; by the Christmas of 1764 she was pregnant, and Henry with impulsive chivalry, or perhaps the honesty of someone who knew he had not long to live, insisted on marrying her.

His father had attempted to pay off the pregnant Mary and her mother with an offer of sixty guineas, but instead the Kidds and Henry left the house. They settled nearby—within an hour's ride—at the village of Ness. Here, Henry, faced with the need to support his imminent family, purchased the freehold and goodwill of the retiring village blacksmith, and set to work at the bellows while he learnt the craft from the former owner. This then was the story behind George Lyons' journey to his lawyer. In making it, while he himself rode out of history, he was securing for the granddaughter he was never to see, a future which doubtless would have appalled him as much as it has intrigued thousands of people for two hundred years. Henry's and Mary's daughter was probably born on 26 April 1765. No precise record of her birth survives, but she was baptised at Great Neston Church on 12 May as Amy Lyons. Earlier biographers have stated that she might well have been from two to four years old at the time of baptism, but the evidence to back these claims is insubstantial. What is certain is that her father died when she was not quite six weeks old, and that his age was a bare nineteen when consumption—abetted by work in the smithy—claimed him.

Mary Lyons took her child to her mother's native village of Hawarden in Flintshire where her relatives looked after them. Mary learnt cooking and sewing and grandmother Kidd taught both herself and her daughter to read and to write. Mary had signed her marriage lines with a mark, and in later life her daughter Amy was often to relate how this fact had pained her, and that she had resolved to acquire all the accomplishments that a wife to someone of Henry's social standing would have had. By the time Amy was thirteen she could read and write—though her spelling was appalling—and cast simple accounts. She was already showing signs that she was to become an outstanding beauty, but at this stage it seems that the dominant facet of her character was the immense closeness she felt to both her mother and grandmother. Over the years gossips and biographers have vilified her as a thoughtless and self-centred adventuress, but they appear to have ignored this side of her character, as well as much else; for Amy retained her pride in and love for her family throughout her life. In the hectic and glittering social life into which circumstances eventually placed her it would have been understandable if she had kept her humble origins in the background. This was never to be the case. Despite the sneers of well-born Englishwomen, her mother lived with her continuously throughout her life, enjoying the same comforts and dignities as her daughter. Neither was the grandmother forgotten. Shortly before the Christmas of 1792, when Amy was Lady Hamilton, wife of the British Ambassador to Naples, and hostess of that city's most glittering salon, she was to write from Caserta to Charles Greville, MP:

'I will trouble you with my own affairs, as you are so good as to interest yourself about me. You must know, I send my grandmother every Christmas twenty pounds and so I ought. I have two hundred a year for nonsense and it would be hard if I could not give her twenty pounds, when she has so often given me her last shilling ... for as the time passes without her hearing from me, she may imagine that I have forgot her. And I could not leave her poor old heart in suspense for all the world... The fourth of November last I had a dress on that cost twenty-five pounds, as it was the gala at court; and believe me, I felt unhappy all the time I had it on.'

At thirteen, Amy reached the age of having to go to work, and the only alternative to fish-gutting, or working on the land or in the Lancashire weaving mills, was domestic service. The Kidd family, as far as Hawarden was concerned, did not work on the land, almost invariably taking positions among the households of the local gentry. With this background Amy had no trouble in securing her first position as a junior nursery-maid in the household of Mr and Mrs Thomas of Hawarden. Mr Thomas, though a qualified doctor, occupied his time farming a large estate. After the squire and the vicar, he ranked third in the Hawarden social scale; he also had good London connections and it was through these that Amy and her mother came to London two years later.

These two years as a junior nursery-maid taught Amy a lot of what life among the gentry was like. Her main functions were to clean the nurseries and prepare the children's meals; she was also responsible for their table manners—such as these were at the time—and occasionally for taking the children down to see their parents in the evening before they went to bed. In this way she sometimes met people who were guests in the Thomases' household. One of these guests was Mr Thomas's brother-in-law, who was an Alderman of the City of London. His name was Bowdell, and he had arrived at the village with a considerable retinue which had attracted a certain amount of attention. Amy's mother had struck up a close acquaintanceship with the Alderman's coachman—a Mr Doggen—and had plans to return to London with him and marry him. Not wishing to split mother from daughter Mr Thomas arranged, through Alderman Bowdell, for Amy to take up a similar position as a junior nursery-maid with a fellow doctor called Budd, of Chatham Place, Blackfriars, a physician at St Bartholomew's Hospital. Dr Budd lived just off Blackfriars Bridge Road and it would be a simple matter in the evenings for Amy to cross over the bridge and visit her mother in East Cheap.

There were in fact other more stimulating things to do. Dr Budd's household was very different from that of Dr Thomas; he kept a large staff and Amy was only the second junior nursery-maid. Her senior was a stage-struck girl called Jane Powell, who in later years was to become one of London's leading actresses. On their days off and with their modest wages of four shillings a week, the two girls would hang around the theatres and other places of amusement. In the London of 1779 theatrical life centred around Drury Lane and the acting profession, though regarded as somewhat bohemian, was heavily patronised by those who had an interest either in the theatre or in the charms of the actresses. Another place of entertainment was further up the river at the 'Ranelagh Gardens'. Here there were puppet shows, ventriloquists, dancing bears, circus acts, firework displays and on Saturdays a masked dance which enabled members of different social strata to mingle as freely as they chose. Between Blackfriars and Ranelagh there were also the more sophisticated delights of the 'Vauxhall Gardens', but here admission alone cost two shillings, so it is unlikely that Amy and Jane Powell ever ventured there.

The only source of information as to the details of Amy's life at this time is one on which no reliance whatsoever can be placed. The *Anonymous Memoirs of Lady Hamilton* was published shortly after her death, and while it achieved considerable notoriety as a scandalous book, and slandered almost everybody concerned with her during her lifetime, it has since been proved to be almost totally inaccurate. In this period of her life she has been credited with working in a shop, working as a hostess in a gambling salon, and working for a variety of tradesmen. However, the only position we are sure about is the one Amy took, as a dresser, with an actress called Mrs Lindley, at the Drury Lane Theatre; and that this position was taken up within three months of Amy going to London and joining Dr Budd's household.

The theatre must have been a heady environment for a fifteen-year-old. At least one early result of this change of occupation was that the homely name of Amy quickly metamorphosed into the more sophisticated Emily. She has been accused of snobbery for this, but a more innocent explanation is equally possible: the Liverpool accent pronounces Amy as Emmy, as anyone who has heard such Liverpudlians as the Beatles will realise. Emmy, of course, is the diminutive of Emily and in the contrived politeness of backstage formality, far more formal than the backstairs social nuances of Dr Budd's or Mr Thomas's household, Mrs Lindley may well have begun to call her Miss Emily instead of Miss Emmy.

Though only fifteen, Emily was rapidly developing the beauty for which she became famous. We know that she had long auburn hair which reached down below her waist, that she was slim, very tall— almost five foot eleven—with long legs but, unfortunately, rather heavy ankles. She spoke with a Liverpool accent and like many Liverpudlians she was possessed of a strong singing voice. Her face, too, must have shown some of that innocence and simplicity which shines through so many of the early paintings that Romney and other artists made of her. Innocent or not she was very shortly to discover the harsher facts of life. There are conflicting stories of her seduction. Most of her biographers grant that dubious distinction to a naval officer by the name of Captain John Willet Payne, later to become a friend of Nelson, a rear-admiral, and the treasurer of Greenwich Hospital. Her seduction has acquired a romantic aura over the years. Apparently a cousin, Thomas Kidd, was taken by the press gang in Liverpool, and his distraught family appealed to Emily's mother to help. Captain Willet Payne was a constant escort to Mrs Lindley and legend has it that Emily successfully appealed to him on her cousin's behalf, and paid for the favour, losing not only her virginity but her job with Mrs Lindley as well.

Equally conflicting are the stories about the outcome of the affair. John Cordy Jeaffreson, who is probably the most accurate of her early biographers, states categorically that she had a child at this time, without being sure of the identity of the father. Two facts are certain: the gallant captain was a friend of Mrs Lindley; and Thomas Kidd was pressed and then released on instructions from London. The time scale alone makes it highly unlikely that she did have a child, but very possibly she had an abortion, because at approximately this period she certainly made the acquaintance of a number of quasi-medical gentlemen; in fact she first came to public notice working for one of them.

Her new employer was a Dr James Graham who dabbled in various medical treatments which were not then, and indeed are still not, wholly accepted by the profession. Graham lectured on hygiene, which was a most creditable thing in those days when even members of the Royal Household were bedevilled by lice in their hair and very rarely took a bath. He advocated mud baths but, curiously, had publicly condemned the newly-fashionable practice of sea-bathing. His favourite ideas were use of the recently-discovered medium of electricity and the efficacy of playing coloured lights on the body. To promote his theories he opened a curious place which he called 'The Temple of Health', or as some of its advertisements styled it, 'The Temple of the Hymen'.

The temple was situated in Royal Terrace, just off the Adelphi at the end of the Strand. Admission cost five shillings, and for this sum one could hear lectures on magnetism, mud baths, coloured lights, and hygiene; perhaps most interesting, while listening to the lectures the gentlemen could observe groups of young ladies wearing just enough clothes not to offend public decency, representing the Goddesses of Beauty, Wisdom and

Health. Emily was one of these goddesses and posed on several occasions as the Goddess of Health.

Upstairs there were rather more expensive attractions and it has been speculated that the Temple of Health was really a rather superior brothel. The most expensive attraction was Dr Graham's 'celestial bed', ostensibly available to married couples who wished to assure themselves of a child. This cost twenty pounds a night. It was also available for fifty pounds a night. Naturally the contemporary advertisements do not specify what extras were included for the extra thirty pounds, but it is unlikely that they included Emily. The popularity of the bed and the Doctor's female assistants ensured a steady stream of the lascivious and the unscrupulous.

In April 1781, just before her sixteenth birthday, Emily attracted the attention of a gentleman called Sir Harry Featherstonehaugh. Sir Harry was the archetype of all the wicked philandering country squires that the nineteenth-century theatre inflicted upon the public. He could have stepped straight out of a novel by Georgette Heyer, for he was young, well built, wealthy, thoughtless, a dashing rider to hounds and surrounded by a group of hard-drinking, hard-riding companions. When he was not in London, he lived at Uppark, which stands proudly on the South Downs with views of Portsmouth and the Isle of Wight. Uppark still stands today and is a fine imposing house built by the architect William Talman shortly before 1700. It was here also that he took Emily when she became his mistress. She was to live with him for almost a year.

Again facts are hard to come by, though there are plenty of legends. We know that Emily learnt to ride and that she rode very well. Legend has it that she presided over numerous high-spirited drinking sessions and she is alleged to have danced naked upon the long dining table. Sir Harry had a liking for girls who were his social inferior and Emily was but one of many who passed through his hands; until he capped his emotional career by marrying one of his dairy maids. Emily herself has written that at this time she led a thoroughly 'giddy life'. Nevertheless she managed to impress one or two people who were visitors to Uppark but who did not take part in the strange goings on. One of these was the Hon. Charles Greville, MP for Portsmouth, who was an occasional weekend visitor; Sir Harry was one of his constituents and commanded a large share of the rural vote.

Charles Greville, the younger son of the Earl of Warwick, was, at the time that he met Emily, a conscientious and popular Member of Parliament. He had proved his worth as a minor official at the Board of Trade and from here he had graduated to a—still fairly lowly—job at the Admiralty. Being the younger son, he had no fortune and his total income came to some £500 a year. This he received from his uncle, Sir William Hamilton, the British Ambassador to Naples. Sir William had recently been widowed and on his wife's death he had inherited her estate at Milford Haven in Wales. He paid Greville this annual income to manage his business affairs during his absence abroad. However, £500 a year was not sufficient to maintain Greville's position, either as a gentleman of some considerable social standing or as a Member of Parliament, even though the duties of the latter occupation were far from onerous. Greville's tastes, whilst they were not extravagant, were most particular. Fortunately his uncle again managed to help him.

Sir William was a notable collector in an age when collecting was one of the most fashionable occupations. The last quarter of the eighteenth century had seen a dramatic rise in the interest that well-to-do Englishmen were taking in the newly discovered sights and legends of classical antiquity. A 'Grand Tour', at least as far as Rome, and preferably to Athens as well, was an essential part of any gentleman's education and few who took this tour returned home without a collection of pictures, bronzes, old master drawings or paintings, both to remind them of their experiences and to impress their contemporaries. Sir William Hamilton had been an avid collector since he was eighteen and his appointment to Naples gave him the opportunity for which he had always longed. He had already formed two major collections of Greek and Etruscan vases and one superb collection of pictures. Today many of his first collection of vases are in the British Museum, while the importance of his picture collection may be judged from the fact that one of his—in his opinion—minor paintings, Velázquez' 'Portrait of Pareja' fetched £1,240,000, a world record price for an oil painting, in 1972. Sir William collected for aesthetic and academic reasons, but in a gentlemanly way he dabbled as a dealer. When young Charles Greville had visited him in Italy some sixteen years earlier, he had soon aroused the young man's interest, and Greville now acted as Hamilton's agent for the disposal of those works of art which were superfluous to the Hamilton collection. Greville's London house in Portland Square was really an antique shop, though everybody was far too well bred to say such a thing. In return for his commissions on the sale of the Hamilton purchases, Greville supplied his uncle with copious background letters giving all the gossip of the Court, Parliament and Whitehall.

Although his interest apparently lay in the antique, Greville was obviously considerably attracted by Emily's rather more modern charms. It is almost certain that he propositioned her in one way or another, though presumably he was too much of a gentleman to try to take her away from Sir Harry. However, when the carefree days at Uppark came to a sudden halt it was to Greville that Emily turned in her distress. She had committed the unforgivable sin and become pregnant, and even more important, she had apparently given Sir Harry sufficient grounds for believing that the child might not be his, though years later he was to accept the responsibility. At the beginning of December 1781 he threw her out of the house with barely sufficient money to travel back to Hawarden, and none to pay the maid whom she had recently acquired.

Back at Hawarden—the object no doubt of curious stares from the villagers, who had seen the girl leave for London in such excitement only sixteen months previously, and now saw her return with some fine clothes, a maid whom she could not pay, and a stomach growing visibly larger every day—Emily sent off several letters to Sir Harry at Uppark. There was no reply.

She also wrote to Charles Greville in London. Greville, prudent and calculating man that he was, had her sent a letter of Christmas good wishes and with it a stock of franked addressed envelopes. It is pure speculation, but was Greville's action part of a contingency plan of his own, or did he feel a degree of responsibility for her condition? Whatever the answer, Greville did in fact accept financial responsibility for the child when it was born. Emily's first letter to Greville was a cry for help, which after thanking him for his kindness in writing to her continued:

'. . . believe me, I am almost distracted. I've never heard from Sir Harry and he is not at Uppark I am sure. What shall I do? Good God! What shall I do? I have written seven letters and no answer. I can't come to town because I am out of money. I have not a farthing to bless myself with, and I think my friends look cruelly upon me... Oh Greville, what shall I do, what shall I do? Oh how your letter affected me when you wished me happiness. Oh Greville, that I was in your position or was in Sir Harry's ... what a happy girl I would have been—girl indeed! What am I but a girl in distress—in real distress. For God's sake Greville write the minute you get this, and only tell me what I am to do ... I'm almost mad. Oh for God's sake, tell me what is to become of me. Oh dear Greville, write to me. Greville adieu, and believe yours forever, Emily Hart. P.S. Don't tell my mother what distress I am in, and do afford me some comfort.'

Greville replied to this letter on the same day that he received it, which is marked as 10 January 1782. At first his answer was circumspect, though it did include an order for sufficient money for her needs and her eventual journey to London. Greville was calculating his odds very neatly, but to Emily, the letter expressed the sentiments of a noble and broad-minded man. He began by saying that her extravagance might have irritated Sir Harry, and reminded her that for the next three months she would anyway be unable to lead 'a giddy life', even if she had wished to. He suggested to her that she should try for a reconciliation with Sir Harry, but in his next sentence dashed these hopes by remarking, 'I don't think a great deal of time should be lost as I have never seen a woman clever enough to keep a man that was tired of her.' After hinting that if she felt no residual love for Sir Harry, then it was a very different matter indeed, Greville came neatly and emphatically to the point: 'If everything fails, if you mean to have my protection, I must *first* know from you that you are *clear of every connection*, and that *you will never take them up again without my consent*. I shall then be free to dry up the tears of my lovely Emily and to give her comfort. If you do not forfeit my esteem perhaps my Emily may be very happy.' He went on to warn her against betraying his confidences and then outlined a plan for the future:

'By degrees I will get you a new set of acquaintances and by keeping your own secret and no one about you having it in their power to betray you, I may expect to see you respected and admired. Thus far relates to yourself. As to the child, Sir Harry may be informed of circumstances which may reasonably make him doubt, and it is not worthwhile to make it a subject of altercation. Its mother shall obtain its kindnesses from me, and it shall never want ... I enclose some money; do not throw it away ... but do not be on the road without money to spare, in case you should be fatigued, and wish to take your time... God bless you, my dearest lovely girl; make your determination soon and let me hear from you.'

Emily clutched at this substantial straw with both hands. When her child was born, a daughter whom she christened Emily and who was handed over to her grandmother to care for, Emily set out for London where she joined her mother. Then Emily and her mother, who improved her name from Mrs Doggen to Mrs Cadogan for the occasion, joined Greville. History does not relate what happened to Mr Doggen.

Greville welcomed them and set them up most comfortably in a small house in Edgware Row just off Paddington Green in north London. In those days this was a gently rural area devoted to market gardening; a quiet stroll of just under a mile through fields and gardens brought them from Paddington Green to Greville's home in Portman Square.

At Paddington Green, Mrs Cadogan did the cooking and Emily had two servants, a maid and housemaid at £9 and £8 a year respectively. The small house was tastefully furnished. Sir Joshua Reynolds' portrait of Emily Berties as Thies hung in the drawing-room, together with a carefully selected group of early Dutch Masters and several folios of fine engravings and mezzotints; there were marble sculptures, bronzes, Etruscan vases—mostly of course on consignment from Sir William in Naples—together with Mr Greville's collections of mineralogical specimens and antique coins. In many ways the house was Greville's 'den' in which he displayed the trophies of his and his uncle's collecting mania. It might be thought that Emily was regarded as just another acquisition. This would not be completely fair as contemporary accounts are unanimous not only in praise of the perfect taste that was everywhere displayed but about the genuine love which Emily and Greville appeared to have for each other.

Greville was proud of his new establishment and it delighted him to invite his 'collecting friends' round for afternoon tea or a quiet drink in the evening. He himself, after completing his work in Whitehall or at the House of Commons, would return to Portman Square, change into less formal clothes and stroll slowly across the fields to Paddington Green where Mrs Cadogan would have his supper ready; afterwards his friends would call and Emily would either entertain them or keep dutifully in the background handing round bumpers of port and sweetmeats. At the same time Greville began his tutelage of Emily, but whether this was part of a long-term plan which perhaps was maturing at the back of his mind, or whether it was merely the Svengali which is said to be in every man, is a matter for conjecture. The first step was easy. Emily was swiftly changed to Emma; secondly Emma was taken to a dressmaker, a Mrs Hackwood, for a wardrobe suitable for the role which Greville wished her to play. For the clothes Greville wrote up a budget of not more than £20 a year, any surplus to be Emma's pocket money. Her spelling was taken in hand. A piano teacher and a singing master were engaged. Emma was instructed to keep all household accounts, and these she had to show to her protector weekly. The total budget was never to exceed £300 a year, and this sum had to cover maintenance for Emma's baby daughter, the rent of the house and all other expenses including Emma's tutors. Any extravagance resulted in a severe scolding.

Emma accepted everything that Greville said, did or planned for her, for she worshipped him for what she considered his goodness, and there is no doubt from her letters and her journals of the time that she was deeply in love with him. Her spelling improved slightly, she mastered the piano, and she learned to talk intelligently about the *objets d'art* which Greville was constantly bringing home. Most important of all, her voice matured and once properly trained developed into a fine mezzo-soprano. One thing that did not change, however, was her cheerful Liverpudlian accent. Emma knew that she talked 'country' and to amuse Greville's friends would play a dialogue with her mother which was almost unintelligible to their cultivated ears. The friends were a congenial and intelligent group, very different from the company at Uppark. They included Sir Joseph Banks, the President of The Royal Society of which Greville was a member; and numerous members of what the members themselves delighted in calling the Society of the Dilettantes. These were gentlemen who had resolved to spend their days, or at least their leisure hours, cultivating the art of pleasure as well as the finer arts. The group also included three painters: Sir Joshua Reynolds, Sir Thomas Lawrence and, from Emma's point of view the most important, George Romney. Most of these acquaintances came to be shown Greville's treasures, including Emma, and would pass their time making knowledgeable remarks about what they saw. Emma must have become used to having her classical features compared to the marbles and bronzes from antiquity that surrounded her.

But Romney meant more to her than all the others; not because they were lovers or had any emotional attachment, but because they had much in common. If Greville had thrown her out, as Sir Harry had done, never to reappear in history, Emma would still be famous from Romney's immortalisation of her in paint. Romney himself came from a humble home in the north of England. His father was a carpenter and small farmer in Cumberland, but noticing that his son had artistic tendencies he had apprenticed him to a minor portrait painter, Christopher Steele. Romney's genius matured swiftly and as soon as he had served his apprenticeship he married and set up business in Kendal. Portrait commissions were most infrequent in Kendal and Romney was sure that the only place for him was London. He left his wife and children in the care of his father and in 1762, at the age of twenty-eight, set out for London with a capital of £50. He opened a studio at Dove Court near the Mansion House, but later moved into Great Newport Street, Soho, close to the studio where Reynolds had begun his painting career. His first success was to win the second prize of 50 guineas which the Society of Arts had offered for a narrative painting. Romney had chosen for his subject the death of General Wolfe, and after he had sold the picture for 25 guineas he quickly obtained many portrait commissions, for which he charged only 5 guineas a time. He worked with almost unbelievable speed and soon found himself earning a more than comfortable living. He saved enough to go off to Italy and spent two years in Rome, Florence and the other major continental cities; then, flushed with somewhat hazy ideas of what the neo-classical age really meant, he returned to London and set up a studio in Cavendish Square. It was here that he attracted the attentions of such patrons as the Duke of Richmond, Admiral Keppel, Lord Lennox, Edmund Burke and eventually Greville's father, the Earl of Warwick.

Romney must have been delighted to have been admitted to Mr Greville's 'den', with all its reminders of classical mythology, but most of all he was dazzled by Emma's looks. By arrangement with Greville it was agreed that Emma should sit for Romney twice a week so that he might paint her in various classical or mythological attitudes. For almost two years Emma's main occupation, when she was not taking singing, spelling or piano lessons, was to sit as Romney's model in Cavendish Square. Greville insisted that she went there and back by carriage and that she was always escorted by her mother. There are no grounds whatsoever for believing the numerous stories scandalously linking Emma with the painter. Romney's son, his biographer William Hayley, and Greville himself are all adamant that the relationship was a platonic one. During this period Romney is known to have painted at least twenty-five portraits of her, and made sketches for many more. He also made a preliminary oil sketch for a portrait of Emma's little daughter.

Romney saw Emma as the epitome of classical perfection, and invented numerous classical poses and attitudes for her. Emma, who had done a bit of posing herself in the not too distant past, proved an apt model, but Romney's own diaries and sketch books reveal that he only sketched her pose and then used another model for the painting itself and for the draperies. Emma was used mainly for her face. The only times that Romney painted Emma using her as a model for the complete picture are his portraits of her as Circe and as Nature. In both cases the poses were discussed beforehand with both Greville and her mother, and Mrs Cadogan was present with her at all the sittings.

The friendship between the fifty-year-old painter and his seventeen-year-old model is not difficult to understand as the two had much in common. They both talked country and came from humble homes. Both felt slightly out of their depth in this relatively sophisticated society; both were highly strung, insecure and dependent on patronage, albeit of a different sort. Romney himself was always tortured by introspection and depression and eventually went mad. Romney became Emma's friend and confidant, a fact confirmed by a remarkable letter that she wrote to him years later from Naples, shortly after she had married Sir William Hamilton.

Naples 1791 [probably late December]

'My dear friend, I have the pleasure to inform you that we arrived safe at Naples . . . I have been presented to the Queen of Naples by her own desire . . . in short I am the happiest woman in the world . . . but why do I tell you all this? You know me enough. You were the first dear friend that I opened my heart to. You ought to know me, for you have seen and discoursed with me in my poorer days. You have known me in my poverty and in my prosperity and I have no occasion to have lived for years in poverty and distress if I had not felt something of virtue in my own mind. Oh my dear friend, for a time I own, through distress my virtue was vanquished, but my sense of virtue was not overcome. How grateful now then I feel to my dear, dear husband, who has restored peace to my mind and has given me honour, rank and what is more innocence and happiness. Rejoice with me my dear friend and my more than father, believe me I am still that same Emma you knew me. If I could for a moment forget what I was, I ought to suffer.'

The sittings for Romney were probably the highlight of Emma's life at Paddington Green, for Grèville could not and would not take her into polite society. Occasionally he took her to the Pantheon to see a play or circus, but her days were mostly spent running the little house, attending her lessons and making sure that all was clean and comfortable for Greville when he came home in the evenings. Even so, the expense of Emma and his new style of life told heavily on Greville's pocket and he was forced to give up the lease of his house in Portman Square. He was quite frank with Emma about his shortage of funds and it would be only natural for her to wonder where her future lay. Then in December 1783, the two of them learnt that

Sir William Hamilton, Greville's uncle, would be staying in London, on leave of absence from Naples, and that he hoped to bring with him one or two highly valuable antiquities which might restore their financial situation.

II

1783–1784

The
Bartered Bride

'. . . I will never be his mistress. If
you affront me, I will make him
marry me.'
Emma to Charles Greville

Sir William Hamilton was a remarkable man, who has
been misjudged by most historians as the classic
complacent cuckold; the acquiescent old fool hovering in
the background of the brilliant relationship of Nelson and
Emma. The facts are different and may be catalogued
swiftly. William Hamilton was born on 13 December
1730, the younger son of Lord and Lady Archibald
Hamilton. At least this is what the records say, and there is
little doubt that Lady Archibald was his mother. However,
before and after his birth she was the favourite mistress of
the Prince of Wales, later to be George II, and he was
brought up as foster-brother to the Prince's son, who in
due course became George III. Thus there is much
circumstantial evidence to suggest that he was a Royal
bastard.

He was educated at Westminster School, and then at the
age of sixteen was commissioned as an ensign in the Scots
Guards. He spent ten years soldiering, seeing active service
in Germany and the Low Countries, and became firm
friends with James Wolfe and Johnny Burgoyne, both of
whom became generals, and who met death and de-
feat respectively at Quebec and Saratoga. Resigning his

commission in 1756, he set about looking for a suitable heiress, and found one in Catherine Barlow, a delicate, plain, sweet-natured girl from Milford Haven in Wales. Years later he was freely to concede to his friends that he had married for money, but of course at that time this was usual. Catherine brought with her a dowry which yielded some £6,000 a year, and for a time the young veteran managed his wife's Welsh estates, developing anthracite mining and drawing up grandiose plans to make Milford Haven a major shipping terminal; a scheme which was not to mature for another two centuries.

Welsh dreams palled but then in 1760, when Hamilton was twenty-nine his Royal foster-brother, who had just come to the throne, made him an equerry; George also needed more support in the House of Commons and so appointed Hamilton to the safe parliamentary seat of Midhurst, Sussex where for four years he was an obedient and loyal member of the King's Party. In due course he received his reward. In 1764 he was offered the post as British Minister to the Court of Naples, which he gratefully accepted: firstly because it was worth £3,000 a year; secondly because Catherine was in poor health, 'dying of an asthma' according to Horace Walpole; and thirdly because Italy was already his spiritual home.

As to the third reason, Walpole has recorded that 'Hamilton is picture mad.' He was quite right. William Hamilton was an insatiable collector, unable to resist buying what he fancied. He had been forced to sell his first collection when he left the army, to avoid being dunned for debts. Now with a rich wife, a comfortable post and a salary to match, he was to live in the country from which had come the pictures he loved. Circumstances and patronage had afforded him the means and opportunity to start new collections.

Hamilton and his wife arrived in Naples on 17 November 1764, and after presenting his credentials, he immediately plunged into the artistic and cultural life of the city. At this time, Naples was second to Paris among European cities both for size and the variety and splendour of its attractions. It had, and indeed still has, probably the finest situation in the world, but though the setting itself was worthy of the finest jewel, the community was sadly flawed. Its nobility was incredibly rich, its poor, known as the *lazzaroni*, pitifully impoverished; the contrast was vivid. Over the whole city hung the shadow of the volcano Vesuvius.

Naples lived on a knife edge of violence, stemming partly from the appalling poverty and the wayward and savage character of the Neapolitans themselves, and also perhaps from the smouldering presence of Vesuvius. Petty quarrels were settled on the spot with a knife. In an early despatch to London, Hamilton reported that there had been five murders on one Sunday morning alone. However, the climate suited Catherine, and shaking off her asthma she became a devoted and active diplomatic wife, gently tolerant of her husband's more obvious peccadilloes and of the way in which he threw himself and her fortune into the pursuit and purchase of antiquities. Her husband was an intelligent man and—unusual for his era—an exceptionally hard-working one. The eighteenth century was a time when a gentleman thought it not only fatiguing but also rather bad form to indulge in any kind of work, except perhaps a little gambling or philandering. Officers of State rarely spent more than a day or two a week at their posts, and together with this aristocratic sloth it was also thought quite unpardonable to show the slightest enthusiasm or display even a modicum of energy in one's chosen occupation.

It was Hamilton's nature to be completely taken up by his interests, and he brought to them great energy and a keen academic mind, as well as an infectious enthusiasm which enabled him not only to make his role as a collector respectable but also to inspire others to follow his example. He brought the same qualities to matters of state, and it was this professional approach which was later to earn Nelson's admiration. Nelson, another unusually active and vigorous man, was to comment after his first meeting with the busy British Minister that 'here was a man after my own heart'.

However, Hamilton's diplomatic successes were as yet a long way ahead, for in the mid-1760s Naples was as much a backwater diplomatically as it was in the mainstream of classical antiquity. The city delighted Hamilton and he threw himself into his new interests with his usual fervour. Vesuvius was his first study and he has considerable claims to be called the first serious volcanologist. He climbed all over the mountain, noting each fissure, each lava outcrop. He recorded its behaviour in all weathers, and was present at the eruptions of 1767, 1779 and 1794. He probed deep into local records, and reported all his numerous observations in a series of letters to Lord Morton, then President of the Royal Society. These caused enormous interest when they were read in London, and two years after his arrival in Naples he was created a Fellow of the Society, a distinction that possibly gave him more pleasure than any other, the more so perhaps since it stemmed entirely from his own unaided efforts. These letters were later expanded by Hamilton and were published at his own expense in 1776, in two volumes entitled *Campi Phlegraei* and subtitled 'Observations on the Volcanoes of the Two Sicilies as they have been Communicated to the Royal Society of London.' A third and supplementary volume followed in 1779. These three volumes are perhaps among the most beautiful books ever produced. Hamilton himself designed the layout, as well as writing the text, and he specially trained a young artist by the name of Pietro Fabris to produce the illustrations under his own personal supervision. Apart from their scientific value, these illustrations are particularly enchanting. Fabris was an Englishman who had settled in Naples and had absorbed the colourful and vivid Neapolitan way of life. His pictures are simple and direct, and on Sir William's instructions are frequently enlivened by the addition of a human figure in the foreground.

The letters and reports which Hamilton sent off to the Royal Society were not confined to volcanoes. His intellectual curiosity took him into fields as diverse as a study of the lightning conductors used on local ships; the existence of a double-headed rose at Paestum; and the habits of the sea snail. He faithfully reported the excavations at Herculaneum, and rapidly acquired the reputation of being one of the most cultured men of his time, and certainly the leader of the Neapolitan cultural scene. What strikes one as being particularly pleasant about his character is that he not only enjoyed scholarship but took great pleasure in passing on his knowledge so that others—particularly artists and scientists—could benefit. There is no doubt, however, that these various activities were costing him rather more money than either he or his wife could afford, for he had not neglected to increase his collection of pictures, and had also soon formed a magnificent collection of Greek and Roman vases, as well as an impressive array of bronzes and other antiquities.

To publicise his first collection he had retained a fellow member of the Society of the Dilettantes, Pierre Hugues, to write an authoritative text alongside engravings of the most important vases. Hugues was an art historian who used the pseudonym 'D'Hancarville', and the four volumes he produced in collaboration with Hamilton had a profound impact on the taste of the time. The volumes were entitled *Collection of Etruscan, Greek and Roman Antiquities from the Cabinet of the Honourable William Hamilton*. Beautiful as they were, Hamilton spent so much money on producing the books that when he came to reckon up he found that he was £6,000 out of pocket.

On his first leave from Naples in 1771, he managed to sell his collection of Greek and Roman antiquities to the newly-founded British Museum for £8,400, and it is this collection which today forms the nucleus of the department of that name. At the same time, with considerable help from Greville, he managed to dispose of over two hundred pictures and smaller items such as medallions, examples of ancient glass, and a substantial amount of antique jewellery. These sales raised enough money for him to pay his debts and start collecting all over again. Hamilton loved collecting for its own sake but he also had a keen eye for objects on which he could make a discreet profit. Like many collectors he could never resist a bargain, and he occasionally got himself into some curious scrapes in his enthusiasm. One contemporary account reports him being seen, in his full ambassadorial regalia, in the back streets of Naples helping a peasant push a barrow laden with his latest purchases. Goethe, on a visit to Naples, recalls being taken down to Hamilton's cellar and there, to his amazement, seeing a pair of fine bronze candelabra, once the pride and joy of the Portici Museum near Pompeii. Goethe was told to keep his mouth shut.

Hamilton's public collection inspired numerous artists; Henry Fuseli and John Flaxman were strongly influenced, but the major legacy that remains with us today is the impression both the vases and the books illustrating them had upon Josiah Wedgwood. Wedgwood had been sent some proofs of the illustrations by Hamilton's brother-in-law, Lord Cathcart, and when Wedgwood opened his new works in 1769, he celebrated the event by issuing a set of six black vases with red enamel decorations taken from figures in Hamilton's book. Since then, figures and designs taken from the decorations on Hamilton's vases have become almost a hallmark of the famous pottery firm. This acceptance by Wedgwood must have pleased Hamilton immensely, as his whole theory of art and, as he publicly claimed, his *raison d'être* as a collector was to influence modern artists and craftsmen. In the preface to the set of four volumes illustrating his collection he had written: 'In every art good models give birth to ideas by exciting the imagination, theory furnishes the means of expressing these ideas, practice puts these means into execution, and this last part which is always the most common is also the easiest.' These words sound somewhat pedantic today, but Hamilton genuinely believed that if by his publications he could improve the art of his time, his work was worthwhile. He did not hesitate to pour scorn on those who collected merely to show off; he even went so far as to train a pet monkey to examine a work of art with a miniature magnifying glass, and to caper about making ecstatic squeaks. He despised the so-called art experts, as common then as they are today.

Looking at this critical side of his nature, it is difficult to reconcile his close relationship with his nephew Charles Greville. In 1769 Greville had visited him in Naples when he was on his own 'grand tour' and the two men, uncle and nephew, had become close friends, regarding each other as equals despite the difference in their ages. They addressed each other as 'My dear Hamilton' and 'My dear Greville' in their letters, but the older man, while he passed on much of his scholarship and introduced his nephew to the society of connoisseurs and artists with whom he was familiar, never managed to imbue Greville with either the enthusiasm or the genuine love that he himself felt for the antique. Greville comes over as a rather cold fish, interested in art for the doors that it opened and the chance of making money from the commissions Sir William paid him.

As time passed, it became clear that Sir William was being passed over for further promotion, and he remained as the British Minister to Naples, although in 1772 his foster-brother George III had created him a Knight of the Order of the Bath. With the exception of two short leaves spent in London, Sir William remained in Naples as its premier diplomat. Affable and scholarly, he became a Neapolitan institution on whom every visitor of consequence to the city felt obliged to call.

Sir William's wife died in August 1782, and the following year he obtained permission to return to England for a year's leave of absence. He had much to do. There was his wife's estate to settle, and as usual he was considerably in debt. He resolved to take with him as many of his antiques as he could bring himself to part with, among these being one work of art which is unique and almost certainly the most valuable item which he was to bring to England. This piece is a vase of Roman cameo glass dating from the time of the Emperor Augustus, though its origins are still surrounded in mystery. Hamilton found it in the gallery of a Scottish antique dealer living in Rome, by the name of James Byres, who in turn had purchased it from the Barberini family after Donna

Barberina Colonna, Princess of Palestrina, had had a series of disastrous losses at the card table. Hamilton paid £1,000 for it and eventually managed to sell it to the Duchess of Portland for 1,800 guineas. It is now known as the Portland Vase and is on exhibition at the British Museum.

To Greville's chagrin, Sir William did not use him as the agent for the sale, although naturally on this visit Hamilton was a frequent visitor at Paddington Green. He was immediately enamoured of Emma. At this time he was fifty-two. He was deeply bronzed, and many contemporaries said that he looked about forty, although here Horace Walpole was an exception, claiming that he had aged considerably and acquired a 'patina'. He was slim, erect, an admirable dancer and a keen sportsman with the reputation of being the finest shot in Europe. In addition he had the worldliness and charm of a gentleman who had spent fifteen years at the Neapolitan court. Emma must have been terrified of meeting him but the courtly Sir William soon put her at her ease.

Emma has left her own account of this meeting which was used by her first serious biographer, Jeaffreson. Certainly the facts make sense and the dialogue rings true. Apparently on first meeting him she thought him an 'old gentleman' and said so to Greville, who expressed considerable alarm and begged her not to say so in his own or anyone else's hearing. It was perhaps a natural response from Emma, for Sir William had been at his most avuncular. After enquiring about the progress of her lessons, he suggested that he be a philosopher and she his disciple so that he could have the honour of instructing her. 'Yes,' he said, 'I shall be your Pliny the Elder and Charles shall be your Pliny the Younger.' Emma's face must have shown that she had not the slightest idea who these Plinys might have been, for Sir William then remarked on several characteristics and experiences which he felt he and the ancient philosopher had in common.

'I am a philosopher and so was Pliny. I am a naturalist, and so was Pliny. Pliny was the author of a great many books and so am I. Pliny had a favourite sister and so have

I. Pliny's sister had a son whom he deeply loved, adopted and made his heir, and so have I.' Both Greville and Emma must have wondered about this last remark, but Sir William continued: 'Pliny went to Misenum and I can claim the same myself. Pliny saw Vesuvius in eruption and so have I, but although he made notes so as to write a book about it, he never wrote it, for the eruption killed him. I've made my notes and I've written a lot but Vesuvius may kill me yet.' He therefore suggested that she call him Pliny and allow him to be her Pliny. On his next call, she took him at his word, and she continued to call him Pliny, except on formal occasions, for years. For his part, Sir William was soon calling her Emma and behind her back 'the fair tea-maker of Edgware Row'.

When he was not attending to his business at court Sir William called most days for tea with his tea-maker, and gently probed Emma as to the state of Greville's finances. These were rapidly becoming rather more than a temporary embarrassment as his creditors were now calling for some £6,000. This obviously made Emma feel desperately insecure, and it is clear from a perusal of her correspondence that she had set out to win Sir William's affection on Greville's behalf. She thought she was succeeding when suddenly, in May 1784, Greville announced that he and Sir William were to undertake a lengthy tour of Sir William's Welsh estates, and he thought it best that she and her mother spend a few weeks in Cheshire, perhaps seeing her daughter, and doing a little sea-bathing. Emma, who was not well—she had developed a form of psoriasis on her arms and knees, a skin rash now acknowledged to result from a nervous condition—believed this to be the signal that he was tired of her. That afternoon, when Sir William called for tea, she suddenly burst into tears.

Sir William dried the tears, and as he later wrote to Greville gave her 'a chaste and paternal kiss'. He assured her that her forebodings were unfounded and that Greville wanted her to bring baby Emma down to London with her on her return, so that the child could be sent to a good preparatory school. But then he added that he had enjoyed her society and, for several weeks now, had drawn a pure delight from the contemplation of her loveliness. Perhaps he might venture to say that he was her devoted servant. Sir William was at his most diplomatic and courtly best, but he spoke relatively innocently because he had resolved that, if his nephew had decided to throw her out, he could well afford to give her a small allowance of say £50 a year. In fact he proposed such a sum to Greville shortly afterwards. Emma's fears, however, were not completely banished by this conversation and she left for Cheshire in a considerable state of worry. One unlooked for result of this conversation, it is reasonable to assume, when Sir William repeated it to his nephew, is that it planted in Greville's mind the seeds of a plan.

Emma and her mother took the stage-coach for the north with some misgivings. Greville had given them 40 guineas, and told them that he would write to them and tell them when his tour was over and they could return. He had recommended Emma to take a course of sea-bathing, and suggested the resort of Abbergely on the Welsh coast. However, having collected the child from her grandmother, Emma wrote to Greville that she had decided not to go to Abbergely as it would be too expensive, and instead they were going to stay at Park Gate, close to Great Neston and the church where she had been christened and her father buried. There they took lodgings with a Mrs Darnwood who provided rooms and board for the princely sum of 35s. a week for the three of them. She herself wrote almost every day, and the letters are those of a girl deeply in love and unsure of her position.

Parkgate, June 15, 1785

'My dearest Greville,

I am in the house of a lady whose husband is at sea. She and her grandmother live together, and we board with her at present until I hear from you. The price is high but they don't lodge anyone without boarding, and it is comfortable, decent and quiet, I thought it would not ruin us till I could have your opinion, which I hope to have freely and without restraint, as believe me you will give it to one who will always be happy to follow it, let it be what it will. As I am sure you would not lead me wrong, my little temper may have been sometimes high, believe me I have always thought you in the right when I have come to reason... So pray, my dearest Greville, write soon and tell me what to do, as I will do just what you think proper; and tell me what to do with the child. For she is a great romp and I can hardly master her. I don't think she is ugly, but I think her greatly improved. She is tall, good eyes and brows, and as to lashes she will be passable. But she has overgrown all her clothes, and I am making and mending all I can for her... Pray my dear Greville, do let me come home as soon as you can for I am almost broken-hearted being from you; but if I was the greatest lady in the land, I should not be happy from you ... indeed my dear Greville, you don't know how much I love you... I don't know what to do ... don't think of my faults Greville, think of my good and blot out my bad for that is all gone and buried, never to come again...'

This time a week passed before she wrote again, and in this period no letter arrived. Emma fell into a fit of dejection and introspection. On 22 June she began a long letter which merits quoting almost in full because no other words could give a truer picture of her mind and emotions throughout this period.

'My ever dear Greville,
    ... Oh Greville, when I think of your goodness, your tender kindness, my heart is so full of gratitude that I want words to express it. But I have one happiness in view, which I am determined to practise, and that is evenness of temper and steadiness of mind ... indeed I will manage myself and try to be like Greville ... I can never be like him. But I will do all I can towards it, and I am sure you will not desire more. I think if the time would come over again I would be different. But it does not matter. There is

nothing like buying experience ... and, oh, Greville, did you but know when I so think, what thoughts—what tender thoughts—you would say "Good God" and "Can Emma have such feeling sensibility? No I never could think it but I may hope to bring her to conviction, and she may prove a valuable and amiable woman."

True Greville! And you shall not be disappointed. I will be everything you can wish. But mind you Greville, your own goodness has brought this about. You don't know what I am. Would you think it, Greville?—Emma—the wild unthinking Emma, is a grave thoughtful philosopher. 'Tis true ... and I will convince you when I see you.

I shall say nothing about this giddy, wild girl of mine. What shall we do with her Greville. She is as wild and thoughtless as somebody when she was a little girl, so you may guess how that is ... Would you believe it, on Saturday we had a little quarrel. I mean Emma and me, and I did slap her on the hands, and when she came to kiss me and make it up, I took her on my lap and cried. Now do you blame me or not? Pray tell me. Oh Greville, you don't know how I love her. Indeed I do. When she comes and looks in my face and calls me mother, indeed I truly am a mother. For she has a right to my protection and she shall have it as long as I can and I will do all I can to prevent her falling into the error her poor once miserable mother fell into ... But it is bathing time, and I must lay down my pen ... I won't finish this letter until the postman comes ... Emma is crying because I won't come and bathe ... adieu until after I've dipped.

Thursday morning

And no letter ... why my dearest Greville, what is the reason you don't write. If you knew my uneasiness you would. You promised ... it is now three weeks since I saw you ... I think that if I could but hear from you I should be happy.

Give my dear love to Pliny and tell him I put you under his care, and he must be answerable for you to me when I see him. I hope he has not fell in love with any rawboned Scotswoman whose fortune would make up for the want of beauty... But don't put him in mind of it for fear... Pray my dear Greville let me go home soon.

The letter continued with a simple argument about the expense of her being away, which was costing slightly over 2 guineas a week. On the Friday morning a letter came from Greville scolding her for extravagance, and reminding her that the only way to deal with a refractory child was by the mother setting a good example. He went on to say that holidays were a mistake for children as it took their minds off other things such as school. However, he followed up this stern admonition with a more friendly letter giving her news of their travels, and remarking how Sir William kept mentioning her and saying how attractive she was. Emma replied, 'Give my kind love to him. Tell him that next to you I love him above anybody and that I wish I was with him to give him a kiss. Don't be affronted Greville. If I was with you I would give you a thousand and you might take as many as you pleased, for I long—I mean I long to see you.'

Greville was to keep her waiting a further five weeks before he and Sir William met her again at Edgware Row. Emma had brought her child with her, and Romney called to see her and began an oil sketch of little Emma. The picture had to be abandoned when the child caught measles, and she had only just recovered when Greville returned. The child, now aged three-and-a-half, was packed off to a dame's school, and for a short while Emma was allowed to have her home on Sundays if Greville was not entertaining. Eventually Greville arranged for another set of foster-parents, and persuaded Emma that it was in the child's interests not to be allowed to call Emma her mother. Instead, a fictional family was dreamt up for her, and thus the situation remained until Sir Harry met his obligations many years later, finding her a place as a governess. In all this Emma acquiesced, although as her letters clearly show, she did so out of a sense of love, duty and gratitude to Greville. He on the other hand, while considerate to her, never seemed by word or action to show any love to her; but then, as he once wrote to Sir William, 'It does not become an FRS to give way to his passion.'

Sir William returned to Naples early in September, but not before he had ordered from Romney a portrait of Emma as a Bacchante, and also helped Greville temporarily to resolve his financial affairs. Greville's creditors agreed to stop harassing him, on condition that he entered into a guarantee for £7,000 which would be payable on his uncle's death. Sir William cheerfully counter-signed the document, but still did not inform Greville outright that he was his heir. Greville had cause for worry because in the social circles in which he moved there was considerable speculation that Sir William might remarry, and until that uncertainty was removed, his own chances on the marriage market were minimal. The King himself had raised this same point, when Hamilton went to take his formal leave before his return to Naples; and, embarrassingly for Greville, in Greville's presence. The King's question was direct: 'Who is to be your heir, Sir William?', following this bombshell up with 'I suppose your nephew Mr Greville.' Hamilton replied diplomatically that this was a question he intended to keep to himself.

From Naples Hamilton advised Greville carefully to study the marriage market, and the delicate position into which he had manoeuvred his nephew, partly through not quashing rumours of his own remarriage, partly through his refusal anyway to state categorically that Greville was his heir, must have given him a certain wry pleasure, for he was well aware of Greville's manoeuvrings on his own behalf. This elegant and, as we would see it today, heartless game of intellectual chess was further spiced when news filtered back to England that Sir William had been paying court to a certain Lady Clarges who was travelling in Italy at the time. Greville promptly wrote to his uncle, enclosing with his letter Romney's Bacchante, which was now finished. Hamilton replied, describing how he had met the lady in Turin, Rome and then again in Naples.

Apparently he had offered her the use of his empty apartments; taking this as a proposal, she had replied that although flattered she had already resolved not to marry again. 'The devil take me if I meant to propose,' wrote Hamilton, 'tho' I own I often have thought that she would suit me well.'

Greville's letter with the Bacchante portrait had been the start of his campaign to transfer Emma from his own bed to his uncle's, on the tacit understanding that his uncle made him his heir. Greville knew that an ambassador had to have the King's permission to marry; and he reasoned that the King would not agree to Hamilton marrying Emma, and that the liaison would effectively dampen any marital ideas that he might have. His first letter was discreetly worded, but it was sufficiently pointed for Hamilton to see where the land lay. After describing how Emma had improved since she had come to live with him, how her character and social graces had developed through his tutelage, he explained that should he find someone whom he had a chance of marrying, he would be 'much harrassed as how to manage or fix Emma to her satisfaction.' A second letter was more direct. He had discussed his uncle's reported affair with Lady Clarges with Sir William's brother, Archdeacon Frederic Hamilton. The Archdeacon disliked the thought of his elder brother marrying again—probably for the same reason as Greville. His advice was that Sir William would be better off by 'buying love ready made'. Abetted by such worldly counsel, Greville wrote at length and as persuasively as possible. He began by gently teasing his uncle about the rumours of his affair with Lady Clarges.

'They say here that you are in love. I know that you love variety and are a general flirt. Some have said that you have the gout. I say I neither know whether your heart or feet are lightest, but that I believe them both sound. I am ... from frequent experience convinced that I can judge for you and you for me ... If you did not choose a wife, I wish the tea-maker of Edgware Row was yours ... I do not know how to part with what I am not tired with, and I do not know how to contrive to go on, and I give her every merit of prudence and moderation and affection . . .'

Greville then tactfully explained that it was only his financial affairs that prompted him even to consider such an idea. He added that he would rather find Emma a comfortable situation now than be forced to dismiss her suddenly if his financial circumstances deteriorated any further. Also she was both too young and too beautiful to be pensioned off back to Hawarden. Apparently he never considered what Emma might have wanted nor did any thought of her child cross his mind.

Sir William's reply has not survived, but it apparently left Greville with a lot more persuading to do. Sir William was no fool and, unlike his nephew, he had considerable respect for other people's feelings. Greville began his next letter by reminding his uncle of his conversation with Emma when he had offered to assist her should the occasion arise. Emma had told him of it, and although Greville knew full well what his uncle's true intention had been, he chose to ignore it and credit him with another motive. 'I tell you fairly,' he wrote, 'that your expression of kindness to Emma and the comfort you promised her in case anything happened to me, made such an impression on her, I concluded that your regard for me had been the only reason for your not making present offers.'

After this pointed remark Greville again went on to list Emma's virtues, and gave some impartial advice on how to handle her. He explained that small and frequent kindnesses were what she treasured most; nor would Hamilton have any need for jealousy, as Emma was quite capable of being faithful and could be trusted with other men. He remarked that she was still only twenty and that her early misfortunes had had an excellent and salutary effect upon her. Having thus pointed out to Hamilton the bargain he would be acquiring, Greville returned to his own affairs:

'If things remain as they are I shall, to be sure, be much

straightened in finances. I shall be whether she remains or not, and literally her expenses are trifling; yet when an income is very small a trifling expense is felt... At your age a clean and comfortable woman is not superfluous and I should sooner purchase it [*sic*] than acquire it, unless in every respect a proper party offered.'

The prospect of Hamilton remarrying obviously terrified Greville: he goes on to assert his opinion that in every respect a liaison with Emma would be preferable to marriage with Lady Clarges, pointing out that the latter's reputation was far from unsullied. In this opinion, he asserted, he was supported by their mutual friends as well as by Hamilton's own brother. Referring again to his conversation with the Archdeacon, Greville continues:

'Your brother spoke openly to me, that he thought the wisest thing you could do would be to buy love ready made, and that it was not from any interested wish, as he was perfectly satisfied with the fortune he had, that it was enough for his family, and that he should be very glad to hear you declare openly your successor, and particularly so if you named me; I write without affectation or disguise, if you find me either reserved or artful you may despise me.'

As the frankness of the letters increases, Greville's desperation becomes more apparent. He again details his financial position and admits that he has hopes of making a proposal to the younger of Lord Middleton's daughters, whom he believes has a dowry of £30,000. He now says quite openly that unless he is his uncle's heir and he can dispose of Emma, then the lady would remain 'inaccessible'.

Possibly it was this last revelation of his real intentions that touched his uncle's heart, for by return of post Hamilton wrote to him confirming that he was indeed his heir, that he had been so for some months, and that his Will confirming this was with his solicitors in Lincoln's Inn. Hamilton explained that he had not intended to tell him this, as life was so changeable, that if for example he had married Lady Clarges, Greville might have been bitterly disappointed to lose an expectation he had taken for granted. However, when Hamilton's letter came around to discussing Emma, it was far more circumspect, showing a consideration for Emma that Greville totally lacked:

'As to Emma, was I in England and you were to bring your present plan to bear and she would consent to put herself under my protection, I would take her most readily for I really love her and think better of her than of anyone in her situation. But, my dear Charles, there is a great difference between her being with you or me, for she really loves you, and could only esteem and suffer me. I see so many difficulties in her coming here, should you be under the necessity of parting with her, that I can never advise it. Tho' a great city, Naples has every defect of a province and nothing you do is secret. It would be fine fun for the young English travellers to endeavour to cuckold the old gentleman their ambassador, and whether they succeed or not would surely give me uneasiness. My regard for Emma is such that if she leaves you and retires to the country, which I suppose she would do were you to marry, I would willingly make her an allowance of £50 a year till your circumstances enable you to provide better for her. I do assure you that when I was in England, tho' her exquisite beauty had frequently its effects on me, it would never have come into my head to have proposed a freedom beyond an innocent kiss whilst she belonged to my friend: I do assure you I should like better to live with you both here and see you happy than to have her all to myself, for I am sensible that I am not a match for so much youth and beauty.'

This is the only letter of Hamilton's which Greville chose to keep, but a study of Greville's letters shows that he did not have an easy task in persuading his uncle. Nevertheless, he persisted. After suggesting that Emma could live in some remote villa, and that perhaps Hamilton could devise some arrangement whereby he could have a trial run to see how the two of them got on together, he concentrated again on acclaiming Emma's virtues.

'She has natural gentility and quickness to suit herself to anything and takes easily any hint that is given with good humour. I have often heard people say you may do anything by good humour, but never saw anyone so completely led by good nature... She may be trusted by you anywhere ... she likes admiration, but merely that she may be valued and not to profit by raising her price. I am sure there is not a more disinterested woman in the world ... all that pleases her is to have that little such as genteel and sensible wear, and of the best quality, and I declare to you that the little excesses which I have experienced were never devoted to follies, but were given to poor relations in the country, for whose care she professes herself grateful, insomuch that I have only to scold her for not having made me supply that demand, instead of making herself bare of pocket money.'

So far, Greville was speaking nothing but the truth, but then sheer dishonesty creeps into his letters as he leads his uncle to believe that Emma is already more than half in love with him, and in her mind has accepted the inevitability of the transfer. Such lies, told to ease Hamilton's conscience, are spiced with more prurient details. 'As I consider you my heir apparent, I must add that she is the only woman I ever slept with, without having ever had any of my senses offended, and a cleanlier, sweeter bedfellow does not exist...'

By the autumn of 1785, Hamilton had capitulated. Led to believe that Emma was inevitably going to lose Greville's affections, and that rather than any other alternative she wished to place herself under his protection from a genuine love and affection for him, he consented to Emma and her mother coming out to Naples to stay with him for a few months. Greville's plan was to tell Emma that he had to spend some months of 1786 in Scotland and that it would be prudent for her not to accompany him. He suggested that she write to Sir William and ask if her mother and she could spend the summer holiday with him, being assured by Greville that he would join them in Naples once his Scottish business was done, to bring them safely home again. At no time did Greville reveal to Hamilton that Emma was more deeply in love with him than ever, willing even to have her child sent to foster-parents so as not to cause him embarrassment. At this stage Hamilton too apparently saw the relationship as merely a summer *divertissement*, a mad-cap adventure such as could only happen in the tolerant ambience of Naples. 'I must confess,' he wrote to Greville, 'that the prospect of possessing so delightful an object under my roof certainly causes in me some pleasing sensations, but they are accompanied with some anxious thoughts as to the prudent management of this business; however I will do as well as I can, and hobble in and out of this pleasant scrape as decently as I can.' Emma and her mother made the overland journey together, escorted as far as Geneva by the artist Gavin Hamilton, arriving in Naples on 26 April 1786, Emma's twenty-first birthday. Sir William met them and installed them in his official residence, the Palazzo Sesso, where he placed a suite of four rooms at her disposal and arranged a constant stream of entertainments. However, Greville's machinations had placed them both on false ground, and Emma's first letter to Greville, dated 30 April shows only too clearly both her bewilderment and the agony in her heart.

'My dearest Greville,

I arrived at this place on the 26th, and I should have begun to write sooner, but the post does not go until tomorrow, and I dreaded setting down to write, for I try to appear as cheerful before Sir William as I can, and I am sure to cry the moment I think of it. For I feel more and more unhappy at being separated from you... For to live without you is impossible. I love you to that last degree that at this time there is not a hardship upon earth, either of poverty, hunger, cold, death or even to walk barefoot to Scotland to see you, but what I would undergo. Therefore my dear Greville, if you do love me, for my sake try all you can to come here as soon as possible. You have a true friend in Sir William, and he will be happy to see you and do all he can to make you happy. And for me, I will be everything you can wish for. I find it is not a fine horse, or a pack of servants, or plays or operas can make me happy. It is you that has it in your power to make me very happy or very miserable. I respect Sir William, I have a very great regard for him, as the uncle and friend of you, Greville, *But he can never be anything nearer to me than your uncle and my sincere friend, he can never be my lover.*

You do not know how good Sir William is to me. He is doing everything he can to make me happy. He has never dined out since I came here, and indeed, to speak the truth, he is never out of my sight. He breakfasts, dines, sups and is constantly by me looking in my face. I can't stir a hand, leg or foot, but he is marking it as graceful and fine; and I am sorry for I cannot make him happy. I can be civil, obliging, and I do try to make myself as agreeable as I can to him, but I belong to you Greville, and to you only will I belong, and nobody shall be your heir apparent.

You do not know how glad I was to arrive here the date that I did. It was my birthday and I was very low spirited. Oh God; that day that you used to smile on me, and stay at home and be kind to me—and that day I should be at such a distance from you! But my comfort is I rely on your promise, and September or October I shall see you. But I am quite unhappy at not hearing from you—no letter for me yet Greville; but I must wait with patience. We have had company almost every day since I came, some of Sir William's friends. They are all very pleased with me; and Sir William is never so happy as when he is pointing out my beauties to them. He does nothing all day but look at me and sigh . . .

You are to understand that I have a carriage of Sir William's, an English one, paintings and new liveries, and new coachman, footman etc.—the same as Mrs Damer had of her own for she did not go with his [Mrs Damer, sculptress, was a former 'friend' of Sir William's]. For if I was going about in his carriage, they would say I was either his wife or his mistress. Therefore, as I am not, and never can be either . . . He told me he had made a Will and left you everything belonging to him. That made me very happy for your sake. Pray my dear Greville, do write me word if you want any money. I am afraid I distressed you. But I am sure Sir William will send you some, and I told him he must help you a little now and send you some for your journey here, and he kissed me, and tears came into his eyes, and he told me I might command anything, for he loved us both dearly; and oh how happy I shall be when I can once more see you my dear Greville . . . You are everything that is dear to me on earth, and I hope happier times will soon restore you to me, for indeed I would rather be with you starving, than from you in the greatest splendour in the world.

April 31

I have only to say I enclose this I wrote yesterday, and I will not venture myself now to write any more, for my mind and heart are torn by different passions that I shall go mad. Only Greville, remember your promise of October, Sir William says you never mentioned coming to Naples at all. But you know the consequences of your not coming for me. Indeed my dear Greville, I live but in the hope of seeing you, and if you do not come here, let what will be the consequence, I will come to England. *I have had a conversation with Sir William this morning that has made me mad.* He speaks—no I do not know what to make of it. But Greville, dear Greville, write some comfort to me. But only remember you will never be loved by anybody like

Your affectionate and sincere Emma

P.S. Pray for God's sake write to me and come to me, for Sir William shall not be anything to me but your friend.'

Greville did not reply. He arranged the transaction with the same social style and accomplishment with which he disposed of one of Hamilton's classical treasures, and in any case he was not in Scotland but making a determined bid for the hand of Lord Middleton's youngest daughter, whom no one had thought worthy of notice until it was rumoured that her dowry might well be between £20,000 and £30,000. He treated a further fourteen letters from Emma, included in the weekly despatches from Naples, with the same cold-bloodedness with which he had parted from her. It can only have seemed natural justice to those who knew of the business that Lord Middleton treated Greville's approaches with an equally studied indifference.

The Bay of Naples is one of the most beautiful places in the world, and it is remarkable that Emma, despite her excursions to Ischia, Capri and Positano, despite the endless series of parties and diversions that Hamilton had arranged for her, should spend her time grieving for Greville; especially when Hamilton had already made it plain that Greville had no intention of joining her in Naples, and that he, Hamilton, was awaiting her pleasure. If Emma had in fact been the wanton adventuress that contemporary opinion and many of her biographers have made her out to be, then her behaviour would have been inexplicable. There are firmer grounds for believing that at this stage in her life she was thoroughly miserable, and that she would far rather have been with her lover at Paddington Green, in spite of her successes in Naples.

For there had been no lack of romantic offers. There was hardly a member of Hamilton's set who had not propositioned her in one way or another. The King of Naples himself had shown his hand soon after her arrival, when he had had his boat rowed over to the foreshore opposite her villa, and with the royal band packed dangerously into a barge, had serenaded her, while he himself sat bare-headed before her, his hat in his hands, his eyes on her face. There had been offers in London as well, but there is no record in either Greville's or Hamilton's personal papers that Emma ever gave either of them cause for jealousy, until over twenty years later when she was to have her notorious but short-lived affair with Lord Nelson.

It was a girl with the men of the Neapolitan Court at her feet who was to write her fourteenth letter to her 'ever dearest Greville'.

'I am now only writing to beg of you for God's sake to send me one letter, if it is only farewell. Sure, I have deserved this, for the sake of the love you once had for me ... you don't know how thankful I shall be for it. For, if you knew the misery I feel, oh! for I love you with the utmost affection... If I don't hear from you ... I shall be in England at Christmas at furthest. Don't be unhappy about that ... I will see you once more for the last time ... oh my heart is entirely broke. Then for God's sake my ever dear Greville, do write me some comfort. I don't know what to do ... I am incapable of anything. I have a language master, a singing master, music, etc, but what is it for? If it was to amuse you, I should be happy. But Greville, what will it avail me?... I have lived with you five years, and you have sent me to a strange place, and no one prospect but thinking you were coming to me. Instead of which, I was told to live you know how with Sir William. No, I respect him, but no never... But no more, I will trust to providence, and wherever you go, God bless and preserve you, and may you always be happy.'

This letter crossed in the mail with one from Greville, which Emma began to answer before she had read the whole of it. It begins with Emma writing that she misses the lips that had sealed the envelope, and then suddenly she explodes. Presumably she had by now read the letter right through, for tucked into the final paragraph is Greville's suggestion that the sooner she climbs into Sir William's bed the better it will be for all concerned.

Emma's reply must have ruffled Greville's feathers, not only by the strength of her anger and scorn, but also by the threat it contained in the postscript.

'As to what you write me to oblige Sir William I will not answer you for oh, if you knew the pain I feel in reading those lines. *You* advise me to go to bed with him. Nothing can express my rage! I am all madness! Greville to advise me!—You, that used to envy my smiles! Now with cool indifference to advise me thus... If I was with you, I would murder you and myself too. Nothing shall ever do for me but going home to you. If that is not to be, I will accept nothing. I will go to London, and there go into every excess of vice till I die.'

She continued in a similar vein, but closed by reminding him that she still loved him, and that she was sure she still held his reciprocal affection. Then she added the postscript: 'It is not your interest to disoblige me, for you don't know the power I have here. Only I will never be his mistress. If you affront me, I will make him marry me.'

III

1784–1791

The
Reluctant Husband

'... amidst other branches of
natural history I have not neglected
the study of the animal called
woman. I have found them subject
to great changes according to
circumstances, and I do not like to
try experiments at my time of life.'

Sir William Hamilton to
Sir Joseph Banks

Emma's intransigence gave both Greville and Hamilton
serious cause for alarm. By the time the Neapolitan
summer had drawn to its stuffy close and autumn had set
in, Sir William was making serious plans for her return,
and had decided to settle £100 a year on her if she went
home. Greville for his part did not want her to return as his
mistress, and had devised a plan whereby both he and
Hamilton would provide her with a small income, while
suggesting that they make George Romney her trustee so
that they could both avoid the responsibility and
embarrassment of having contact with her. Sir William,
perhaps regretting his part in the whole sordid transaction,
insisted that Emma should be consulted, and it is obvious
from his letters that he felt that Greville had compromised
and misled both him and Emma. Greville in his turn
continued to offer advice to his uncle, and professed to
have a clear conscience over the whole affair. Greville

suggested that Hamilton should try and find some attractive man to take her off their hands, but cautioned that 'the difficulty will be to reject improper offers . . . at any rate she will have the good sense not to expose herself with any boy of family; she must look to someone from twenty-five to thirty-five, and one who is his own master.' However no likely lover appeared, and from the tone of Emma's correspondence it is clear that she had no intention of seeking one out. But even at this stage Greville had not entirely given up hope for his original plan, and he continued to encourage Hamilton to press his suit even harder. 'I have often told her,' he wrote, 'that I never expected from a woman a power to withstand favourable opportunity and a long siege.' He advised Hamilton not to take her temper too seriously, as it was usually caused by hurt pride and anxiety about her future; Emma had obviously been giving Hamilton the rough edge of her Liverpudlian tongue.

As part of a last attempt Hamilton decided to change his approach, and his new ploy was worthy of someone who combined a diplomatic background with the mind of a classical scholar. He had long had the curious habit of paying young boys to come and swim in the nude on the beach opposite his villa, and in a letter to Sir Joseph Banks at the Royal Society had gleefully confided how he had encouraged his pet monkey to pinch their private parts. Now a letter from Greville gave him an idea which chimed in with these somewhat voyeuristic tendencies in his nature; Greville had written: 'Emma's passion is admiration, and it is not troublesome because she is satisfied with a limited sphere but is capable of aspiring to any line.' He mentioned her series of poses for Romney, and how naturally she had assumed the poses Greville and the artist had decided upon. He continued: 'It would be indifferent when on that key, whether she was Lucretia or Sappho, or Scaerola or Regulus; anything grand, masculine or feminine, she could take up . . .'

Hamilton had an open-fronted chest constructed, sufficiently large for someone to stand up in. The inside was painted jet black, and the outer edge surrounded with a magnificent gold frame. Emma was persuaded to pose inside it, first as a human replica of figures from classical mythology, and later, it can be fairly surmised judging from the colour scheme of the chest, as representing some of the figures from the antique paintings from Pompeii, which Josiah Wedgwood had used on his black basalt vases. On the rare occasions that these figures are clothed, they wear only a piece of ochre-coloured chiffon. It seems fair to assume that the near-nudity of Emma's poses gradually led to the intimacy which Hamilton so much desired; though she had withstood a long siege, Emma now began to give way to Sir William, and shortly before the Christmas of 1786 she became his mistress. His happiness was only matched by Charles Greville's relief.

Soon Emma had accepted the situation, and being an impulsive and open-hearted girl she set about loving and cherishing Sir William with the same fervour which had hitherto been reserved for Greville. On Christmas day Sir William had to leave her suddenly. They had planned a quiet Christmas together in his small country villa at Caserta, but the King of Naples had requested Sir William's presence at a hunting party; this being a Royal command, Sir William had to go. Emma sent him a letter by messenger, and there can be no mistaking her feelings.

'Pray don't scold me for writing to you, for indeed I can't help it ... certain it is I love you and sincerely, and indeed I am apprehensive too much for my own quiet, but let it be. Love has its pleasures and its pains; for instance, yesterday when you went away from me, I thought all my heart and soul was torn from me, and my grief was excessive I assure you; today I am better *perché*? The day after tomorrow is Friday and then I shall have you with me to make up for the past pain. I shall have much pleasure and comfort, and my mind tells me, you will have much pleasure to come home to me again ... I shall receive you with smiles, affection and good humour, and think that had I the offer of crowns I would refuse them and accept you, and I don't care if all the world knows it . . .'

Sir William was besotted by Emma; he never tired of having her painted or sculpted, but also devised other more curious ways of showing her off. He sent to Greville for some scarves, and with some simple props devised a series of poses or tableaux known as the 'Attitudes'. These were not for his private pleasure but for semi-public consumption. The German poet Goethe, who stayed with them during the spring of 1787 when Emma had been Hamilton's mistress for only three or four months, was one of the first to see their little exhibition. He has left a vivid description of it in his book *Italian Journey*.

'Sir William Hamilton who still lives here as Ambassador from England, has at length, after his long love of art, and long study, discovered the height of these delights of nature and art in a beautiful young woman. She lives with him; an English girl of about twenty years of age. She is very handsome with a beautiful figure. The old knight has made a Greek costume for her which becomes her extremely. Dressed in this, letting her hair fall loose, and making use of a couple of shawls, she exhibits every possible variety of pose, expression, and aspect, so that in the end the spectator almost imagines himself in a dream. Here one sees in perfection, in ravishing variety, in movement, all states of mind flow rapidly one after another. She suits the folding of her veil to each expression with wonderful taste, even adapting it into every type of headdress. The old knight holds the light for her and enters into the exhibition with his whole soul. He thinks he can see in her a likeness to all the most famous antiques, to the beautiful profiles on Sicilian coins—yes, to the Apollo Belvedere itself! This much at any rate is certain, as an entertainment it is quite unique. We saw it on two evenings with complete enjoyment.'

When the two lovers were not wholly engrossed with each other, they busied themselves redecorating Sir William's villas at Caserta and Posillipo, and supervising the work on what was then, and is today, called the 'English Garden'. This was an enterprise which had been started by the Queen of Naples, who had asked Sir William's advice. He in turn had written to his old friend Sir Joseph Banks, who had sent out a talented landscape gardener called Graffer. The Queen supplied about fifty acres of land, and a staff of eighty together with the money to make the garden. She herself soon lost interest in the project, but fortunately for posterity the King developed a sudden passion for horticulture, and Sir William and Emma were drawn into the project. Graffer was to remain a friend of Emma's to the end of her life, but at this time he was to lean heavily on her to interpret for him, ease his money problems, and to seek redress on his behalf when the Neapolitans cheated him. Sir William delegated much of the organisation to her as well, but it was time well spent, for five years later Emma was to write what a favourite place it had become for both themselves and the royal family. 'The King and Queen go there every day. Sir William and me are there every morning at seven o'clock, sometimes dine there, and always drink tea there. In short it is Sir William's favourite child, and both him and me are now studying botany, but not to make ourselves pedantical prigs and show our learning like some of our travelling neighbours, but for our own pleasure...'

Sir William also wrote numerous letters about the garden, mostly to Sir Joseph Banks, on one occasion remarking coyly that the 'pretty plant he had transplanted from England was doing famously'. In fact the pretty plant was universally admired, even the King's brother, the Duke of Gloucester, complimenting Sir William on 'your little friend about whom I have heard such enchanting reports'. Her first year with Sir William had been very different from her years at Paddington Green, yet in some ways she still gently pined for Greville. However, it was not until August 1787 that she began to write to him. The first letter was an omnibus one, taking her almost four months to write, and it tells us very clearly of her feelings and the life she was leading.

'Although you never think me worth writing to, yet I cannot so easily forget you and whenever I have had any particular pleasure, I feel as though I was not right, until I had communicated it to my dearest Greville. For you will ever be dear to me, and although we cannot be together, let us correspond as friends. I have a happiness in hearing from you, and a comfort in communicating my little stories to you, because I flatter myself that you still love the name of that Emma, that was once very dear to you, and, but for unfortunate evils, might still have claimed the first place in your affections. And I hope still, you will never meet with any person that will use you ill. But never will you meet with the sincere love that I showed you. Don't expect it; for you cannot meet with it ...

We have been at Sorrento on a visit to the Duke Saint de Maître for ten days. We are just returned. But I never passed a happier ten days except in Ed .. re R .. d.

In the morning we bathed, and returned to a fine summer-house, where we had breakfast. But first this summer-house is over the sea, on a rock that looks over Capri, Ischia, Procheza, Vesuvius, Portica, Naples, etc., the sea all before us, that you have no idea of the beauties of it from this little paradise. After breakfast we viewed the lava running down three miles of Vesuvius, and even now and then black clouds of smoke, rising into the air that had the most magnificent appearance in the world. I have made some drawings from it, for I am so used to drawing now, it is as easy as A B C. For when we are at Naples, we dine every Sunday at the Villa Emma at Posillipo, and I make two or three drawings. Sir William laughs at me, and says I shall rival him with the mountain now.

After breakfast I had my singing-lesson; for Sir William has taken a musician into the house. But he is one of the best masters in Italy. After my lesson we rode on asses all about the country, paid visits, and dined at 3.00, and after dinner sailed about the coast, returned and dressed for *conversazioni*. We had Sir William's band of music with us, and about dark the concert in one room, and I sat in another, and received all the nobility . . . Last night I sang fifteen songs. One was a recitative from an opera at St Carlo's. The beginning was '*Luci Bell sio vadoro*', the finest thing you ever heard, that for ten minutes after I sang it, there was such a clapping, that I was obliged to sing it again . . . I left some dying, some crying, and some in despair. Mind you, this was all nobility, as proud as the devil. But we humbled them . . .

Sir William is very fond of me, and very kind to me. The house is full of painters painting me. He has now got nine pictures of me, and two a-painting. Marchant is cutting my head in stone, that is in cameo for a ring. There is another man modelling me in wax, and another in clay. All the artists come from Rome to study from me, so that Sir William has fitted up a room, that is called the painting-room . . .

Sunday Morning. We were last night up Vesuvius at twelve o'clock, and in my life I never saw so fine a sight. The lava runs about five miles down from the top; for the mountain is not burst, as ignorant people say it is. But, when we got to the hermitage, there was the finest fountain of liquid fire falling down a great precipice, and as it ran down it set fire to the trees and brushwood, so that the mountain looked like one entire mountain of fire. We saw the lava surround the poor hermit's house, and take possession of the chapel, notwithstanding it was covered with pictures of saints and other religious preservatives against the fury of nature. For me, I was enraptured. I could have stayed all night there, and I have never been in charity with the moon since, for it looked so pale and sickly; and the red-hot lava served to light up the moon, for the light of the moon was nothing to the lava. We met the Prince Royal on the mountain. But his foolish tutors only took him up a little way, and did not let him stay three minutes; so, when we asked him how he liked it, he said "*Bella ma poca roba*", when, if they had taken him five hundred yards higher, he would have seen the noblest, sublimest sight in the world . . .

I must tell you I have had great offers to be first woman in the Italian Opera at Madrid, where I was to have £6,000 for three years. But I would not engage, as I should not like to go into Spain, without I knew people there. And I could not speak their language. So I refused it... Galini has been here from the Opera House at London to engage people ... I certainly shall sing at the Pantheon and Hanover Square, on the condition Galini has proposed, which is £2,000...

It is a most extraordinary thing that my voice is totally altered. It is the finest soprano you ever heard, so that Sir William shuts his eyes and thinks one of the castratos is singing; and, what is most extraordinary is that my shake, or trill, what you call it, is so very good in every note, my master says that, if he did not feel and see and know that I am a substance he would think I was an angel ... Sir William is in raptures with me. He spares neither expense nor pains in anything. Our house at Caserta is all newly fitted-up for me—a new room for my master, a music-room for me. I have my French master; I have the Queen's dancing-master three times a week; I have three lessons in singing a day—morning at eight o'clock, before dinner, and in the evening; and people make interest to come and hear me...

But last night I did do a very extraordinary thing. We gave yesterday a diplomatic dinner. So after dinner I gave them a concert. So I sent the coach and my compliments to the Banti, who is first woman at St Carlo's, and desired her to come and sing at my concert. So she came, and there was near sixty people. So after the first quartet, I was to sing the first song. At first I was a little frightened, before I began; for she is a famous singer, and she placed herself close to me. But when I began, all fear went away, and I sang so well that she cried out, "Just God, what a voice!" In short, I met with such applause that it almost turned my head. Banti sang after me, and I assure you everybody said I sang in a finer style than her ... Sir William wanted to show me off to some Dutch officers with a sixty-gun ship and a frigate. The commodore, whose name is Melville, was so enchanted with me that, though he was to depart the next day, he put it off, and gave me a dinner on board, that really surpasses all description. First Sir William, me and mother went down to the mole where the long boat was waiting—all man'd, so beautiful! There was the commodore, and the captain and four more of the first officers waited to conduct us to the ship. The two ships were dressed out so fine in all the colours; the men all put in order; a band of music and all the marines did their duty, and when we went on board, twenty pieces of cannon fired. But as we passed the frigate, she fired all her guns, that I wish you had seen it. We sat down thirty to dine,— me at the head of the table, mistress of the feast, dressed in all virgin white and my hair all in ringlets, reaching almost to my heels. I assure you it is so long, that I really looked and moved amongst it; Sir William said so.

That night there was a great opera at St Carlo's, in honour of the King of Spain's name-day. So St Carlo's was illuminated, and everybody in great gala. Well, I had the finest dress made up on purpose, as I had a box near the King and Queen. My gown was purple satin with white satin petticoat trimmed with crepe and spangles. My cap lovely, from Paris, all white feathers. My hair was to have been delightfully dressed, as I have a very good hair-dresser. But for me unfortunately, the dinner on board did not finish till half-past five, English. Then the Commodore and officers would have another bottle to drink to the loveliest woman in the world, as they called me at least. I whispered to Sir William and told him I should be angry with him, if he did not get up to go, as we were to dress, and it was necessary to be at the theatre before the Royal party. So at last they put out the boat, to offer a salute from the two ships of all the guns. We arrived on shore with the Commodore and five principal officers, and in we all crowded into our coach, which is large. We just got in time to the opera. You must know this letter has been begun about four months, and I have written a little at a time, and I now finish from Caserta, where we have been five weeks. We go to Naples on the 28 of this month,

December, and stay till the carnival there, and then return to this place. I believe we shall have a great eruption soon; for though we are here sixteen miles from Naples, yet yesterday the mountain made such a dreadful noise, just like cannons in one's ears: Sir William and me were yesterday, as indeed we are every day, at the Queen's Garden; and whilst Mr Graffer and me were talking, all of a sudden there rose such black columns of smoke out of Vesuvius, attended with such roaring, that I was frightened, and last night I went on the leads of our house here, and the glow was such, that I could see Naples by the light of the fire very plain, and after the glow the red hot cinders fell over the mountain. The Cavaliere Gatty, who arrived here yesterday and is to come to stay with us a week, says the day before yesterday he spoke with Padre Antoine, an old priest, who lives on the mountain, who told him that in a week or fortnight a mouth would open the Portice side, and carry all that place away. At least, there is bad signs now.

I took last night one of my maids, who is a great bigot, to the top of the house, and I showed her the mountain. But, when she saw the great fire, she fell down on her knees, and cried out, "*Oh Janaro mio, Antonio mio.*" So I fell down on my knees and cried aloud, "*Oh Saint Coala mia, Coala mia.*" But she got up in a hurry and said, "*E bene Signora la vostro Excellenza non credo in St Janaro evero.*" So says I, "*No Teresa evero per . . .*" She looked at me, and said to be sure I read a great many books, and must know more than her. But she says, "Does not God favour you more than us?" Says I, "Non." "Oh God," says she, "your excellenza is very ungrateful! He has been so good as to make your face the same as he made the Blessed Virgin's, and you don't esteem it as a favour?" "Why," says I, "did you ever see the Virgin?"—"Oh yes," says she, "you are like every picture that there is of her, and you know the people at Ischia fell down on their knees to you, and begged you to grant them favours in her name."—And Greville, it's true that they have all got it in their heads I am like the Virgin, and they do come to beg favours of me.

Last night there was two priests who came to our house, and Sir William made me put the shawl over my head, and look up, and the priest burst into tears and kissed my feet and said "God had sent me a purpose." Now as I have such a use of shawls, and mine is worn out, Sir William is miserable. For I stand in attitudes with them. Pray write to me and tell me, if I shall sing at the Opera or not. We shall be in London this spring twelve months. We are going to Rome this spring. Adio and believe me more your friend than what you are to me.

Emma.

P.S. I send you a kiss on my name. Its more than you deserve. Pray give my love to your brother, and compliments to Legge, Banks, Tollemache, etc. Tell them to take care of their hearts, when I come back. As to you, you will be utterly undone. But Sir William already is distracted in love, and indeed I love him tenderly. He deserves it. God bless you!'

Sir William was not quite so distracted as Emma thought; he too was writing regularly to Greville and although he confirmed Emma's reports of her social successes, and her rapid progress at music and languages, he was well aware that Emma had marriage at the back of her mind, and he hastened to reassure Greville on that point. '. . . she would be welcome to share with me, *on our present footing*, all I have during my life, but I fear her views are beyond what I can bring myself to execute.' He went on to say that once Emma realised this, she would undoubtedly make them both unhappy, and that possibly they would separate. If this did occur, he proposed to settle £150 a year on Emma and £50 a year on her mother. He added '. . . but all this is thinking aloud to you and forseeing that the difference of fifty-seven and twenty-two may produce events; but indeed hitherto her behaviour is irreproachable, but her temper, as you must know, unequal.'

Emma certainly had a temper, but she was also developing a remarkably strong character. As she grew more confident of her position, so her feelings for

Hamilton changed from respect to genuine and possessive love for him. In no way whatsoever did she ever give him a chance to doubt her fidelity, and in turn she kept him from the amorous adventures that had so grieved his first wife. In court circles, which were probably the most amoral in Europe, she was totally accepted as being not only a very beautiful woman, but a very moral one as well. As her influence increased, she began to drop hints that in fact Sir William and she were already secretly married, and it was only his diplomatic position that made it impossible to announce the fact publicly. In this campaign she had an ally in the Duchess of Argyll, who stayed with them in Naples for a few weeks. The Duchess was a cousin by marriage to Sir William, and she promised Emma that she would do all she could to further her cause, both with Sir William and, more important, with King George himself.

These rumours of a secret marriage seeped back to England and Sir Joseph Banks, who probably heard of them through the reports sent to him by Graffer, the gardener, wrote to Sir William asking the truth of the matter. Hamilton's problem was that he could not marry without the King's permission, and at that stage this was highly unlikely. To do so would mean forfeiting his job. However he was honest to Banks about his feelings and the following letter placed them firmly on the record.

6 April 1790
'To answer your question fairly, was I in a private station, I should have no objection that Emma should share with me *le petit bout de vie qui me reste* under the solemn covenant you allude to, as her behaviour in my house has been such as to gain her universal esteem and approbation, but as I have no thought of relinquishing my employment, and whilst I am in a public character, I do not look upon myself at liberty to act as I please, and such a step I think would be imprudent and might be attended with disagreeable consequences. Beside, as amidst other branches of natural history I have not neglected the study of the animal called woman. I have found them subject to great

changes according to circumstances, and I do not like to try experiments at my time of life. In the way we live, we give no scandal, she with her mother and I in my apartment, and we have a good society. What is there to be gained on my side? It is very natural in her to wish it, and to try to make peole believe the business done, which I suppose has caused the report in England. I assure you that I approve of her so much that if I had been the person that made her first go astray I would glory in giving her a public reparation, and I would do it openly, for indeed she has infinite merit, and no princess could do the honours of her Palace with more care and dignity than she does those of my house. In short, she is worthy of anything, and I have and I will take care of her in proportion as I feel myself obliged to her; but as to the solemn league, *amplius considerandum est.*'

Then he added a paragraph which can be taken two ways. Either it asks Banks to scotch the rumours that were floating about London, or perhaps it asks him to make his personal feelings clear to those close to the King. 'Now my dear Sir, I have more fairly delivered you my confession than is usually done in this country, of which you may make any discreet use you please. Those who ask out of mere curiosity I should wish to remain in the dark.'

The curious remained in the dark until the following year when Sir William and Emma came home on leave, Hamilton's first for seven years. He had much to do, and to the consternation of Greville the two of them lived together quite openly. They had travelled overland, visiting Venice and Vienna on the way, and on their arrival in England, Emma was to score yet another series of successes. Her 'Attitudes' enchanted a great many influential people. The Duchess of Devonshire described them as 'perfect—everything she did was just and beautiful!' Lord Charlmont found them 'a new source of pleasure to mankind', whilst Horace Walpole, meeting her at the Duke of Queensberry's house at Richmond, described her singing as 'admirable' and her attitudes as a 'whole theatre of grace'. At the end of August, Sir William was sent for by the King at Windsor, while Emma waited at home, doubtless wondering what the verdict would be. The King received his old foster-brother courteously and told him that though the Queen could not receive Emma formally as his wife, he himself had no objection if he wished to marry her. Hamilton returned home, and though he still had some private reservations about the marriage, his own sense of fair play prevailed and he formally asked Emma to marry him.

In all her excitement, Emma did not forget her old friend George Romney. Out of fashion and ill, he had almost given up painting, for he suffered badly from depression. Emma called on him, teased and rallied him, and promised to come whenever she could to sit for him as she had in the old days. He immediately started his portraits of her as Joan of Arc, as Mary Magdalene and as a Bacchante, all commissioned by the Prince of Wales. Romney was delighted with the gesture and the patronage that followed it, telling his friend and biographer Hayley that she was a 'divine woman'. 'I cannot give her any other epithet, for I think her superior to all womankind.'

The wedding was at Marylebone Church on 6 September 1791. It was conducted by Edward Barry, the Vicar of Elsdon, Northumberland, and the witnesses were Lord Abercorn and a Mr Dutens, who was the secretary to the British Minister at Turin, and a close friend of them both. After the ceremony the two of them entertained their friends to a breakfast before catching the weekly packet from the Tower, to France and Paris for their honeymoon. One man was conspicuously absent from the celebrations: Charles Greville was allegedly making arrangements for little Emma, still fostered out. Neither he nor Emma cared to mention this matter to Sir William.

IV

1791–1795

The
Queen's Messenger

'Lady Hamilton . . . is a young
woman of amiable manners . . .
who does honour to the station to
which she is raised . . .'

Captain Horatio Nelson, RN,
to his wife

France was a smouldering volcano, with Paris as its crater.
The National Assembly had been in power since the
storming of the Bastille two years before, but Louis XVI
and his Queen, Marie Antoinette, were still the heads of
state, though in little more than name. The shops and
amusements seemed unchanged, the balls and parties
continued as before and neither Sir William nor Emma
seem to have remarked on the undercurrents of
resentment, epitomised by the puritanical dress of the
deputies who together with the Tricolour of the
Revolution dominated the city. Instead, both of them were
delighted to receive a summons to be presented to Marie
Antoinette. The summons was doubly welcome: Emma
had not been allowed to attend the English Court, and
therefore still could not be formally presented at the
Neapolitan. However, Marie Antoinette was a Habsburg
and the younger sister by three years of Queen Maria
Carolina of Naples. What Queen Charlotte of England
refused to do, Marie Antoinette more than made up for.
She gave Emma the social *cachet* she needed, and ensured

her reception in Naples by asking her to carry a secret letter
to her elder sister. The Royal audience and the Royal letter
removed the last lingering doubts as to their position in
Naples. Sir William and his lady journeyed casually the
length of France, and thence down to Naples via Rome,
delighted with each other and oblivious of the political
holocaust that was soon to burst upon them. Sir William
had not always been so blind to the state of nations. In fact
his strictures upon the society of Naples and the behaviour
of the Court had on several occasions delighted the Foreign
Office. But he had never been one to interfere; life after all
had much more interesting things to offer than social
change, and though Sir William could recognise tyranny
and corruption when he saw it, he believed almost
religiously that improvements should come from the
governing classes.

This was one reason why he had been such a
conspicuous success at the Neapolitan Court, which would
have had little time for a meddler or reformer. Naples had
already been a Spanish province for generations when in
1700 Carlos III of Spain created his third son, Ferdinand,
its King. Ferdinand was eight years old at the time, and
though untouched by the insanity which afflicted his
brothers was decidedly simple. It was largely by design
that the King was almost totally lacking in education, as his
tutors and doctors had decided that should he ever be
presented with any difficult problem, the mental effort
involved in coming to grips with it would probably topple
him over the brink to join his brothers. He grew up with
childish tastes, enjoying pinching his courtiers' bottoms,
and delighting in defecating in public after a meal. He
loved hunting and fishing, but had not the slightest interest
in government—or in any form of Court ceremony. He
was never happier than when catching fish in the bay with
the peasants of Naples, and then selling his catch at his own
stall in the market place, haggling, swearing and jesting
with all and sundry. Next to fishing he liked shooting. The
Royal shoots were a particularly disgusting form of
organised slaughter, at which Ferdinand would insist on

gutting the animals and showing their entrails to everybody on the shoot. He was a close friend of Hamilton mainly because, as has already been mentioned, Hamilton was an expert shot. His lack of connection with the corrupt Government of the day and his cheerful vulgarity endeared him to the riff-raff of the city, the *lazzaroni*. Not unnaturally he was cordially despised by the aristocracy, the intellectuals and the middle classes.

Carlos tried on three occasions to marry Ferdinand off to one of Maria Theresa of Austria's daughters, eventually succeeding in 1768 when Ferdinand and Maria Carolina were married. Maria Carolina was as clever as her husband was stupid. She let Ferdinand go his own way, and outwardly was a dutiful wife (the marriage produced seventeen children). But in no time she had gathered the reins of government into her own hands, reducing the Spanish connection to next to nothing. She allowed her husband to amuse himself as he wished and ruled Naples herself in medieval style, caring little for what her ministers did in the Royal name so long as they drummed up sufficient money from the population to pay for Royal expenditures. The most important government official was General Sir John Acton, an English-born Catholic who had spent his life abroad, serving in the French forces and later as an administrator in the Austrian Court. He was a man who talked a lot about reform but who did very little about it. Instead he seized every office for himself so that there would be no one to oversee or audit his actions. Beneath him, government officials wallowed in a bath of corruption, secure in the knowledge that Acton would never have either the time or the energy to interfere.

Anger and resentment bubbled beneath the surface. The poor hated their poverty, the intellectuals saw only too clearly the moral bankruptcy of their own country, while many of the nobility were sickened by the constant round of dissipation and avarice which stemmed from the Royal Court. Acton had recently succeeded to an English baronetcy, rather to his own surprise. Many in Naples saw this as an English bribe to persuade Naples to side with

England against the might of France and Spain. In fact the baronetcy was hereditary and had nothing to do with the complex politics of the time, in which every European nation watched the revolutionary posturings of France, and jockeyed for position.

The message which the French Revolution gave to both the intellectuals and the masses of Europe was not the heady blend of Liberty, Fraternity and Equality which its leaders preached. It was simply the chance of a change, for almost any change would have to be for the better. Europe had outgrown the medieval style of monarchy, though there were many, Maria Carolina for one, who did not agree.

At this period much of Sir William's time was being taken up by the sixth son of George III, the Prince Augustus, later the Duke of Sussex, who was on a long visit to Naples. Sir William had been warned from London that the Prince was as amorously inclined as his eldest brother, the Prince of Wales, and great care had to be taken to circumvent his more dubious activities. He was one of a long succession of notable English visitors who had decided, because of the political troubles in the rest of Europe, to spend their long holidays and winters in Naples, still considered a political backwater safe from the taint of revolution. Many of these visitors had to be entertained, and several had to be presented at Court because of their social rank. Emma, whom the Queen had received with every kindness and some show of affection, had charge of presenting the ladies, and apparently behaved herself thoroughly well. In the lull before the gathering storm Sir William's and Emma's life was as sociable, amusing and interesting as ever. Sir William even had the time to start cataloguing his second collection of vases, the last major undertaking for which he would have liked to be remembered. This time the catalogue was in four volumes, which appeared between 1791 and 1795. They were not so sumptuously produced as the first volumes had been, but they served the same useful purpose. 'I wish,' wrote Sir William, 'that Wedgwood had this collection two years in his possession, he would profit much...' The engravings were made by the German artist Wilhelm Tischbein, who was Director of the Neapolitan Academy of Painting, and the completed work was called *Collection of Engravings from Ancient vases, mostly of pure Greek workmanship discovered in Sepulchres in the Kingdom of the two Sicilies.* Many of the vases were later to be lost at sea during a shipwreck, but the engravings have survived and one look at any collection of Wedgwood will show that Sir William was right.

Gradually however the influence of the French Revolution began to undermine the pleasures of scholarship and social life. The first disagreeable sign was the arrival of a Monsieur Mackau, the newly-appointed French envoy. Technically he had been appointed as the representative of Louis XVI, but this was a fiction which fooled no one, as Louis was virtually a prisoner. Monsieur Mackau was a Republican to the backbone, and lost no time in making his feelings obvious. The Queen, desperately worried about the position of her sister Marie Antoinette, at first refused to receive him, and when on 24 August 1792 she and Ferdinand were prevailed upon to do so, the reception was chilly. Within the month France had declared itself a Republic, and Monsieur Mackau went so far as to appear at the San Carlo Opera House wearing the uniform of the French National Guard, a studied insult to the Queen.

The whole business placed Sir William in a very delicate position. For some years he had been the doyen of the diplomatic corps in Naples, and as such it was his duty to smooth out such lapses of etiquette. Then Monsieur Mackau went even further, tearing down the French Royal coat-of-arms from his official residence and replacing it with the symbol of the Revolution, the red cap of liberty. No one was more relieved than Sir William when he caught what he thought was a slight chill, so that he could get out of Naples and retire with Emma to his villa at Caserta to recover. Unfortunately the chill settled on his liver, and for fifteen days he was dangerously ill, with

Emma spending days and nights at his bedside throughout the crisis. Thereafter Sir William preferred to remain at Caserta to convalesce, a period which he almost certainly prolonged as much as he could so as to avoid being involved in the embarrassments which were now an everyday occurrence in and around the Court.

The Queen, frantic about the safety of her sister and apprehensive about the future of her Kingdom, decided that as close a relationship with England as possible was the course to follow. Because of Sir William's illness, she used Emma as her go-between, sending her twice-daily notes of encouragement, condolence and advice, together with gifts of flowers and medicines. An extraordinary relationship now grew up between the twenty-six-year-old Emma and the forty-four-year-old Queen. Polite and respectful in public, Emma had use of a secret back stairway to the Queen's apartment, and was in the habit of spending an hour or so *tête-à-tête* with her most evenings. Napoleon maintained that lesbianism was at the root of it, but this is almost certainly untrue. The most probable explanation is that the Queen, largely confined to her private apartments, where Sir William, even if he had been up and about, would have been unable to visit her with propriety, had decided to use Emma as a tool in order to get the English support she desired. Emma in her turn was immensely flattered and proud of her role. As Greville had written not so long before, 'her passion is admiration'. As the Queen's confidante, Emma became a power to be reckoned with in the Court circles. In December 1792, with Sir William almost completely recovered but still diplomatically convalescing at Caserta, a French fleet sailed into the Bay of Naples; its sole intention appeared to be the humiliation of the Queen. The presence of the fleet gave open encouragement to the machinations of Monsieur Mackau, and many Neapolitans who hitherto had been wary of proclaiming their sympathies for reform now came out into the open. The French fleet stayed for only a day and a night, but hardly had they left when a severe storm drove them back again. King Ferdinand was forced to throw open the facilities of the Royal dockyards in order to get the ships repaired as quickly as possible, and thereby get rid of them. The French Admiral repaid this gesture by delivering a final insult: on 12 January—the King's birthday—he held a banquet aboard his flagship, attended by all those who professed Jacobin, that is, pro-Revolution, sympathies. It was a convivial affair; the assembled company sang odes to the glories of liberty, and consumed two thousand litres of wine (never paid for) which was drunk to the toast of 'Death to the Tyrant'. The French fleet's sails were still visible on the skyline when word arrived from Paris of the execution of Louis XVI.

The Queen was horror-stricken and immediately the Royal Family went into the deepest mourning, which, characteristically, Monsieur Mackau refused to wear. Queen Maria Carolina, pregnant again, was now even more concerned for her sister's safety, and she redoubled her efforts to bring about an English alliance. Fortunately for her, on 1 February 1793, without consulting the Neapolitans, France declared war upon England.

The French threat had driven Maria and her ministers to realise that some degree of reform was essential, however undesirable they might personally have thought it to be. The declaration of war now gave them their excuse for delaying any such reform or modernisation until the end of hostilities. Sir William, in his first despatch since he left his sickbed, reported accurately to London:

'To the best of my judgement His Sicilian Majesty, accustomed to a life of continued dissipation, gives but little attention to the affairs of state, which are transacted chiefly by the Queen and General Acton... The Queen is by no means popular, but as her power is evident, is greatly feared. No one doubts of the capacity of the integrity of General Acton but they complain, and I fear with some reason, that having taken upon himself almost every department of state, he has not time (tho' a perfect slave to business) to transact the half of which he has undertaken, and which, being left to the corrupt clerks in his office, causes much clamour and discontent.'

Sir William went on to explain the suspicions that many Neapolitans had over Sir John Acton's recent baronetcy and concluded:

'The Neapolitans have certainly an utter aversion to the French, but the late transactions in France have opened their eyes. They are now sensible that in this country justice does not exist, that the government is very defective, and that the people have a right not to be trampled on. So that if this government does not speedily and seriously set about reform in all its branches, the general discontent now silently brooding will probably, sooner or later, break out into open violence. Nature has done more for the Kingdom of the Two Sicilies than for any other kingdom in Europe, and yet I have been witness myself of more misery and poverty among the inhabitants of some of its richest provinces than I ever saw in the whole course of my travels.'

Having duly made his report, which in itself was a scathing indictment of the system in which he lived and the Court which he served, Sir William did nothing more about it. On instructions from London he continued to support Ferdinand, and immediately began negotiations with Acton for an alliance between England and Naples. His instructions came directly from London by King's Messenger, the first time that Sir William had been accorded this privilege, and the first time he had ever been obliged to conduct diplomatic negotiations of any serious consequence. The treaty was concluded on 12 July 1793. Among other clauses was Britain's agreement to protect the Neapolitan merchant fleet, provided there was no trade with France, and Naples' agreement not to make a separate peace with France without Britain's consent, and if that consent was obtained she was thereafter to maintain a strict neutrality. Most important of all, and in order to keep her side of the bargain, Britain agreed to maintain a fleet in the Mediterranean while hostilities continued, provided that when required Naples would supply six thousand troops and twelve ships for the joint campaign against France.

Britain's first move against France was a premature one. The city of Toulon had not endorsed Republican principles, and with the consent of the City Fathers Lord Hood, the Commander-in-Chief of the British Mediterranean fleet, had occupied the city at the end of August. The Republicans had immediately besieged the town and Lord Hood urgently needed reinforcements. Under the treaty, these were available from Naples, and the Commander-in-Chief sent one of his more energetic post captains to that city. This was Captain Horatio Nelson, RN, in command of HMS *Agamemnon*, who arrived in Naples on the evening of 11 September 1793. The following morning, after completing a careful toilet, he was rowed ashore.

The King received him enthusiastically; after the humiliations which the French fleet had inflicted upon them, any British man-of-war would have been welcome. General Acton produced the troops, which Ferdinand paraded with himself marching at their head. Maria Carolina did not meet Nelson, as she was in the last stages of her pregnancy as well as being ill as a result of her grief for her sister. Nevertheless it may be safely assumed that she heard every detail of the visit, if not from her ladies-in-waiting or Acton then from the ever-willing Emma.

For diplomatic reasons Sir William decided to make an exception on this occasion.

In all his time at Naples he had never entertained an officer in his house unless he was of the nobility, but now he had to show both Naples and Lord Hood that he was taking the emergency seriously. He invited the young Nelson to stay at Palazzo Sessa, giving him the room which until recently had been occupied by Prince Augustus. Nelson spent only four days ashore, and almost every hour was taken up with conferences, attending to the administrative details necessary to embarking four thousand troops, and waiting upon a King who treated the whole affair as a game. He can have had very little time even to see Emma. Emma anyway was busying herself translating the sheaves of documents and forms with which the Royal Navy, even in those days, insisted on burdening its officers; and what spare moments she did have, she spent showing Nelson's young midshipman-stepson, Josiah Nisbet, the sights of Naples.

In return for the civilities shown him, Nelson invited King Ferdinand to dine aboard the *Agamemnon*, and Sir William graciously sent over the food and wine for the banquet, as men-of-war were not equipped for entertaining kings. Luckily for Sir William's cellar and his pocket, the banquet was cancelled when news was brought that a French ship was in the area and Nelson decided to give chase. He returned Sir William's provisions, and was not to see either Naples or the Hamiltons again for almost five years.

Biographers and historians have made much of this first meeting, some saying that it was here that Nelson and Emma first fell in love. In fact Emma hardly noticed him, though in later times she was to claim she had. Sir William had liked the active and ambitious young man, who appeared to get things done in much the same way as he had himself in his younger days. Nelson, meeting someone who was obviously prepared to put himself out on his behalf, who had caused him to be entertained by Royalty, and who had helped him so admirably in achieving Lord Hood's wishes, was extremely grateful. Whatever the bond between the two men, it was based on mutual respect, and for the next five years Nelson was to be a regular correspondent of Sir William's.

It is worth looking a little more closely at the character and background of the young Nelson. At this time he was thirty-five. He was not a hero, though he had seen a considerable amount of active service, mostly in the West Indies and Nicaragua. For the last five years he had been on half pay, living in his father's Norfolk parsonage with his plain but affectionate wife whom he had married in the West Indies. This was Fanny Nelson, the widow of a doctor called Nisbet, who, when Nelson met her, was living quietly on the island of Nevis with her young son. She was a middle-class woman, with solid values and an unbounded faith in her new husband. But stepson Josiah was a surly young man who hated the sea and had little respect for his stepfather. He dared not show his feelings openly, and appears to have displayed them much as any 'mixed up' and rejected child would today. He seems—or so the Navy records and Nelson's letters imply—to have concentrated on doing everything he could, short of open rebellion, to embarrass his stepfather.

Nelson himself was small and sickly to look at, and, though it is impossible to diagnose specific complaints at a remove of almost two hundred years, was probably an epileptic. His physical condition had been seriously weakened by fever caught in South America, but he was carried forward by an almost obsessive desire to be a hero. He claimed to have had a vision when a young midshipman that if he put his trust in God, then God would in due course and in some mysterious way make him famous. At this period God had yet to oblige. Nelson, now on his way to Toulon with the Neapolitan reinforcements, was to write from his cabin to Fanny at home in Norfolk:

'I have acted for Lord Hood in such a manner that no one could exceed and am to carry from the King [of Naples] the handsomest letter in his own handwriting that could ever be penned. This I got done through Sir William Hamilton and the Prime Minister [General Acton] who is an Englishman; knowing how much it would please the Lord [Lord Hood] he will get soon also I think a handsome present. Lady Hamilton has been wonderfully kind and good to Josiah. She is a young woman of amiable manners who does honour to the station to which she is raised. . .'

The letter and the present had been solicited by Nelson in order to curry favour with Lord Hood, and Hamilton, sensing the ambition in the young man, had persuaded King Ferdinand to write it; to be more precise, to copy it out from Hamilton's and Acton's draft in French. It took an uncommon amount of time, as Ferdinand could barely write his own name, but it served Nelson's purpose, and in due course the present of a diamond-encrusted snuff-box arrived to gratify Lord Hood.

The Toulon expedition was a disaster and eventually Lord Hood had to evacuate the city, leaving behind some six hundred Neapolitan casualties. When the Republicans entered the town they promptly slaughtered over six thousand Royalists. The Neapolitan survivors trickled back to the city, their stories of the inefficiency of .the campaign and the horrors they had undergone inflaming opinion on both sides. At the same time came the news of the execution of Marie Antoinette. The Queen, driven into a frenzy by grief and a desire for vengeance, looked about her for some group on which to vent her feelings and picked on the members of the middle classes and the intellectuals who had pressed for reforms and who had been entertained by the French fleet, those supporters of Republican France in their midst. Three were promptly executed, and almost a hundred arrested, taken to the dungeons of the Castel St Emo and forced to dig their own graves. This done, each was chained to a stake in his separate hole, and left to rot. Those who survived did so due to the secret kindnesses of their friends, who included many of the jailers and the officers of the fort.

As if these events were not trouble enough for the long-suffering Neapolitans, Vesuvius now lent her contribution to their misery. On 11 June a major earthquake shook the city, and black clouds gathered overhead making it almost impossible to distinguish night from day. Three days later the eruption began in earnest, to last for almost two months. The belching fire and lava did not erupt from the cone, but burst from the mountain's sides. When it was over it was seen that the old cone and summit had completely disappeared, leaving the mountain smaller than the nearby Mount Somma which it had hitherto dominated. Sir William, ignoring his age and his weakened constitution, followed every facet of the mountain's activity, and in due course sent to the Royal

Society a detailed account which again earned him considerable praise.

Hamilton describes how as many as fifteen jets of flame and lava burst from the volcano's sides, completely destroying the towns of Resina and Torre del Greco. Great red stones were flung high into the air, to crash down on Naples itself. One which Sir William measured was thirty-five feet across and ten feet thick. The weight of the ashes that settled on Naples was sufficient to cause several buildings to collapse. 'It is impossible,' he wrote, 'that any description could give an idea of this fiery scene or of the horrid noises that attended this great operation of nature. It was like a mixture of the loudest thunder with incessant reports, like those from a numerous heavy artillery accompanied by a continued hollow murmur like that of the roaring of the ocean during a violent storm.' When the eruption eventually ceased, three thousand acres of vineyard had been devastated and the cathedral of the ruined town of Torre del Greco was buried beneath forty feet of lava.

Initially the populace thought that the noise was caused by a French bombardment from the sea, and they gathered in their thousands at Caserta, armed with anything they could lay their hands on to defend their country. When they realised it was Vesuvius, the patriotic fervour turned first to panic, thence to penitence, and characteristically thereafter to looting. To control the crowds the Cardinal Archbishop summoned them to the Cathedral of St Januarius, in which was housed a golden statue of the saint, together with phials said to contain his blood. On important days the phials were brought out, and the solidified blood would liquefy when held up to the people. A Neapolitan legend said that during the great eruption of 1631, the statue and the phials had been held up before the onrushing flow of lava which had threatened to engulf the city, and the lava had stopped. Now the same scene was repeated, but this time the lava took a course into the sea, where it boiled fish alive, increased the coastline at one point by some 1,000 feet, and melted the pitch between the planks of the boats.

By the end of July 1794 it was safe to make a cautious inspection of the mountain, and Hamilton made his sixty-eighth ascent, observing that some of the craters were half a mile in circumference. After one more minor eruption on 25 August, the mountain was still, and Hamilton wrote down his graphic account, and commissioned seven views and maps, which in due course were engraved by the Royal Society. When Hamilton had finished, Emma celebrated the occasion by having a miniature painted of him.

With Vesuvius quiet and the Royal vengeance satisfied, the Neapolitan Court, headed by its extraordinary Royal Family, and seemingly unaffected by the fall of Toulon and the growing French power in Italy, again took up its pleasurable activities. Many Englishmen took advantage of the phoney peace to return to the city, including the Prince Augustus and some of Sir William's more colourful relations and friends. One such was Frederick Hervey, Earl of Bristol and Bishop of Derry. The Earl Bishop was a highly eccentric, bisexual gentleman who took his religious duties remarkably lightly. He arrived in Naples wearing a crimson velvet coat, slashed with a black sash embroidered with silver. Purple stockings and a white ermine hat completed the picture which certainly impressed the *lazzaroni*, who imagined him to be some kind of English pope. His Borgia-type appearance was enhanced by a profusion of jewelled ornaments ranging from crucifixes to rings, every one outdoing that of the most ostentatious cardinal, capped by an exquisite miniature which he wore around his neck on a gold chain. The miniature however was not of some saintly figure but of the Countess of Lichtenau whom he liked to claim was his mistress. This was somewhat presumptuous on his part, for the good lady in question was very firmly the mistress of King Frederick of Prussia. Nevertheless, despite his many eccentricities the Earl Bishop was a firm friend of the Hamiltons, and a regular correspondent with both Sir William and Emma. Now he wrote to thank Emma for her latest letter, and to invite himself to stay with them at Caserta. 'You say nothing of the adorable Queen; I hope she has not forgotten me ... I verily deemed her the very best edition of a woman I ever saw—I mean of such as are not in *folio* and are to be had in *sheets*.' Emma invited him to stay for a fortnight and the Queen, to whom no doubt the somewhat *risqué* compliment had been passed on, invited the Hamiltons and their guest to dinner in her private apartments.

The Earl Bishop's behaviour was as alarming and occasionally as embarrassing as his appearance, but however much he scandalised the company he was in, he was immediately forgiven. On one memorable occasion he almost over-reached himself. The Hamiltons were giving a concert in honour of Prince Augustus, who had returned to bother Hamilton with his whims and follies, and to celebrate the occasion they had engaged Mrs Billington, then the most famous English singer, to perform. Carried away by the music, the Prince started to join in the songs. The audience was stoically enduring the Prince's total lack of tone, when the Earl Bishop thundered at him to shut up, as 'you have the ear of an ass'. Nevertheless, the Prince continued. Afterwards the Bishop commented in the Prince's own hearing: 'Very fine braying but intolerable singing.' The main reason for this eccentric cleric's visit to Italy was to collect works of art with which he intended to furnish the palatial house he was building for himself at Ickworth, in Suffolk, and he spent many happy hours closeted with Sir William discussing his latest acquisitions. His letter of thanks after he left gives an enchanting picture of the Hamilton ménage: 'Oh how I long to stretch myself in my garret at Caserta, and hear all your excellent anecdotes and dearest Emma's Dorick dialect; eat woodcock pie and quaff humble port.'

Another visitor was Sir Gilbert Elliot, later to become Lord Minto and a friend and observer of Emma and Lord Nelson, who noted down his impressions of both Emma and the Queen. He considered that Emma, who had always been a tall woman, had grown enormously and appeared to be growing every day—in all directions at once. He thought her face beautiful but her character, though pleasant and open, rather spoilt by an incessant need to please and to be admired. Privately he noted that though she had 'a considerable natural understanding' and was 'excessively good humoured' her cheerfulness and spontaneity were those of a good barmaid. On the other hand, he thought the Queen had a strong powerful mind and was full of 'courage, vigour and firmness'; he had no doubt that what she wanted she would achieve.

These perceptive notes go a long way to explain why Emma was now to fall so completely under Maria Carolina's spell. Her wish to please and win admiration had been ingrained in her by both Greville and Sir William, and though her face was still considered beautiful, and still frequently likened to that of the Virgin Mary, she was bitterly conscious of her figure. In fact she was showing the first symptoms of the dropsy which was eventually to assail her. The Queen, seeing how dependent upon Emma Sir William had become, and now desperate to tie England even closer to Naples, continued to work upon Sir William through his wife. Here she was again fortunate. Both Sir William and Emma contracted a mild form of dysentery, from which Emma swiftly recovered; but Sir William, now sixty-five and weakened by his fever of the year before, took longer and was still bedridden by the middle of April 1795 so that the Queen had plenty of chances for private contact with Emma.

V

1795–1798

Under
the Rose

'Before this time tomorrow, I
shall have gained a peerage or
Westminster Abbey.'
*Rear Admiral
Sir Horatio Nelson*, KB,
on the eve of the Battle of the Nile

The Queen opened her campaign subtly. As with Sir
William's previous illness, there were twice-daily
messages of comfort, but this time she made a point of
flattering Emma as well. Emma, frightened that she was
going to lose the husband whom she had grown to love,
must have been feeling more than her usual sense of
insecurity. The smart English travellers had all left for
home; now the only news she gathered was of Napoleon's
continued success in Europe and, despite the Queen's
severe measures against it, the growth of pro-French
opinion in Naples itself. Her response to the Queen's
letters was capitulation: she became her devoted and
unquestioning tool. As she put away the Royal letters in
her lettercase, she endorsed many of them with the
sentiments that she was feeling at the time; these letters
together with her comments survive today, and through
her flowery language her sentiments are obvious. 'From
my ever dear respectable and adorable Queen of
Naples... Oh that everyone could know her as I do!
They would love and esteem her as I do from my soul.' In

her turn Maria Carolina was asking questions such as how Sir William had passed the night, and sending quinine with a note saying that she would 'fain keep you company; my friendship might comfort you.'

The Queen did more than write. She gave Emma one of her equerries, dressed in the Royal livery, to escort her about the city and between the Hamilton villa and the Palace. She provided pedigree horses from the Royal stables for her to ride, their saddle-cloths emblazoned with Sir William's arms alongside those of the Royal household. At the same time she pumped Emma for news from the English Court, and through her succeeded in passing her messages and policies over to London, despite the fact that officially it should have been King Ferdinand who briefed Hamilton on such matters. The Queen's use of Emma conveniently bypassed the King and many of the officials whom the Queen suspected of being hostile to her anti-French policy. The King, who left to himself would infinitely have preferred to remain neutral, had recently yielded to opinion within the Court and recalled the very pro-British and anti-French Neapolitan Ambassador to England, the Count Castilciala. This had annoyed George III, who had accused Sir William of losing his diplomatic touch. The following letter from Emma to Greville written at this time shows how involved Emma had become both with Sir William's official duties and with the Queen.

'I write in a hurry as I have a vast deal to do and the Queen has just sent to me that a courier is to go off for England this afternoon. Poor Sir William has been in bed eight days with a bilious fever and was better, but would get up yesterday which has thrown him back and today he is not so well, but the doctor who is in the house with me says there is no danger. I am very uneasy and not well myself as I have not been in bed since he was taken ill. He was always subject to bilious attacks, but after this illness I hope he will be better than he has been for some time for the quantity of bile he has discharged these past days is incredible and he is naturally of a strong healthy constitution. We are going to get good saddle horses as we live much in the country; riding will do him good and is very good for bilious complaints. You never answered my letter by the last courier nor sent me what I wanted, so I will not trouble you with any more commissions, but try to find out somebody else who will be more attentive to me. My ever dear Queen has been like a mother to me since Sir William has been ill; she writes to me four or five times a day, and offered to come and assist me; this is friendship. I have seen letters that the King of England is not pleased with this Court and Sir William because they did not leave Castilciala with them. Sir William did all he could and he does not care whether they are pleased or not, as they must be very ungrateful to a minister like him that has done so much to keep up good harmony between the two Courts and has done more business in one day than another would have done in ten, owing to the friendly footing he is on here with their Majestys and ministers, so if they are out of humour they may be, but between you and me, I have spoken a great deal to the Queen about the consequence it is to them to have a person of Castilciala's abilities and being beloved in England there and I believe he will return from a letter I had from the Queen this morning; and yesterday she said they would do their utmost, but I can assure you Sir William did all he could to have him kept in England, so don't let them blame the best and most worthy man living, for they have no minister like him.

I have had Lady Bath with me here two days. I carried her to the Queen. She is very shy, but she took a great fancy to me as I put her at her ease and did the honours of a ball for her that she gave at Naples. She invited all the Neapolitan ladies of the first distinction and I was to present them and she took a nervous fit and would not come out of her room for three hours. At last I got her out and brought her into the room between me and Lady Berwick and I carried the ladies who were dancing one by one to her in a corner and she took such a liking that we are very great friends. You were to have married her, I think I heard. However, the Queen was very civil to her as she is to everybody I carry to her. I have had a very bad bilious fever this winter, near dying, but it was owing to fatigue when Prince Augustus was with us, dancing, supping etc, etc, etc. Send me some news, political and private for against my will owing to my situation here I am involved in politics and I wish to have news for our dear much loved Queen, whom I adore nor can I live without her, for she is to me a mother, friend and everything. If you could know her as I do how you would adore her, for she is the first woman in the world, her talents are superior to every woman's in the world and her heart is the most excellent and strictly good and upright, but you will say it is because I am so partial but ask everybody that knows her. She loves England and is attached to our Ministry and wishes the continuation of the war as the only means to ruin that abominable French council.

Ever yours
Emma Hamilton'

King Ferdinand was not the only monarch to be both bored and frightened by the war. The French had over-run the Netherlands and England was now at war with Holland. Spain, which was technically allied to England against the French, began to scent danger if she stayed in the alliance; Carlos IV, King of Spain and Ferdinand's elder brother, began to make secret approaches to the French asking for a separate peace, at the same time asking the French to protect Ferdinand's throne. On 2 April 1796 he wrote a most secret letter in cypher to Ferdinand revealing his plans; the Queen filched it from his pocket and sent it to Emma with a note: 'I send you a letter in cypher from Spain,' she wrote, 'which you must return to me before twenty-four hours so that the King may find it again. There are some very interesting facts for the English government which I am delighted to communicate to them, to show my attachment to them and my confidence in the worthy Chevalier whom I only beg not to compromise me...' The Chevalier was her name for Sir

William, but in fact it was Emma who was now the unofficial Ambassadress. The fact that the Queen sent the letter in cypher shows that either Sir William or Emma had already obtained the key, and almost certainly they got it from the Queen. There were many other such letters throughout this period, and frequently the Queen gave Emma verbal messages for Sir William to embody in his despatches. Emma was now acting as secretary and translator, for as her husband conceded, she now both spoke and wrote French and Italian better than he did.

There have been numerous attempts by biographers of both Emma and Hamilton to play down Emma's diplomatic activities throughout this period, some even stating that she wholly invented her role. However, many of the documents still exist, perhaps the most impressive being a copy of the truce agreement King Ferdinand eventually made with the French. This is still preserved among Sir William's posthumous papers, dated the same day as the agreement and accurate in every detail. It is also in Emma's handwriting. On top of this piece of evidence it is also known that the terms of the agreement were not formally conveyed to Sir William by the Neapolitans until some three weeks after its completion. The truce had been forced upon Ferdinand. The armies of revolutionary France had invaded Italy and were already in Milan and preparing to march on Turin and Genoa. In England, the harvest had been poor, food was short, and many banks had failed. Mutiny was brewing in the fleet. Corsica had been abandoned to the French, dislodging Nelson from his base, after having cost him the sight of his right eye in the siege before Calvi. Now the Admiralty evacuated Malta as well and withdrew the fleet from the Mediterranean altogether. Spain—as foretold in the letter which Emma had brought from the Queen—made peace with France and declared war on England. England preferred a neutral Naples to one allied to France and encouraged Ferdinand to negotiate, Nelson alone standing out for a fight. 'If Naples must fall,' he wrote to Hamilton, 'let it fall as it ought, defending itself to the last.' However, Ferdinand secured a humiliating truce, and paid a vast indemnity. Maria Carolina was forced to release her political prisoners but she retained her policies, writing covertly to Emma that Naples was 'nominally neutral but never in our feelings'.

The French were certainly aware of such sentiments, and did their best to stifle them. In January 1797 they demolished the Austrian army at Rivoli, and by March the Pope had been forced to cede Bologna, Ferrara and Romagna to France; other north Italian states were quickly gobbled up. In October Austria succeeded in coming to an uneasy peace by signing away Belgium and Lombardy to the ever-growing Napoleonic Empire. By the end of the year Napoleon was eyeing Rome. Just after Christmas a young French officer was accidentally shot in a quarrel outside the French embassy and Napoleon, seizing this as an excuse, sent General Berthier with his army into the city. The Pope, Pius VI, was eighty years old and seriously ill. French troops burst into his apartments, ripped off his bandages to make sure of his identity, and then sent him into exile. Rome was declared a Republic, as the French were within two days' march of Naples itself. The Neapolitan Kingdom was now the only neutral or non-French-dominated state on the Mediterranean's European coastline. Napoleon's grand design was almost complete, for he now had the way clear to Africa and Egypt, with his rear flanks secure when his Army embarked, and no port available to succour or replenish the English fleet, which would have to operate from Gibraltar.

The English fleet had not been idle, troubled by mutiny though it was. There had been open rebellion at the Nore and Spithead, and the spirit of mutiny had permeated as far as the Mediterranean fleet under Sir John Jervis, which was now blockading Cadiz. Nelson, one of Sir John's commanders, had four of his seamen court-martialled and executed, hanging them from the yardarm on a Sunday morning. He ignored protests that traditionally Sunday was not a day of execution, remarking that if it had been Christmas Day he would have used a headsman. Fortunately for the fleet, any further thoughts of mutiny

evaporated when Sir John sighted the Spanish fleet off
Cape St Vincent on the evening of 13 February 1797. The
following day was to see the battle which earned Sir John
the earldom of St Vincent, and in which Nelson first came
to public notice.

The Spanish fleet consisted of twenty-seven ships which
were sailing in two groups, one of seventeen and one of
ten. Sir John, who had only fifteen ships, decided to attack
and destroy the seventeen before the other ten could arrive
thereby making the contest hopelessly unequal. Naval
tactics of the day were for ships to be formed into a 'line of
battle' so that their guns could be fired on either side
without damaging each other. To leave the line of battle
was a court-martial offence.

Sir John formed his line and steered for the gap between
the Spaniards, who were at right angles to his bows. As he
entered the gap, he signalled that when the last English ship
was through the gap they were to tack to their left, and
through the Spanish line; however, the Spaniards began to
close the gap faster than was anticipated, and if they had
succeeded the English fleet would have been left astern of
the whole Spanish line.

Nelson, commanding HMS *Captain* (74 guns) was No.
13 in the line. He saw that unless something were done Sir
John's tactic would fail. Without orders, and risking court-
martial, he turned his ship out of the line, threw it into the
gap, and began to engage both the Spanish groups
simultaneously. Sir John saw and approved Nelson's
action, and immediately ordered other ships to support
him. In the ensuing *mêlée*, the Spanish ships thoroughly
roasted the *Captain*, shooting away all its ropes, spars and
sails, and damaging its steering. At the same time they
were blinded by the smoke from their own and Nelson's
guns, and began firing into each other. The *San Nicholas*
(84 guns) and the *San Josef* (112 guns) collided, becoming
hopelessly entangled. Nelson put the *Captain* alongside the
San Nicholas while Captain Sir William Parker boarded the
San Josef. After a further brief *mêlée* on board, the *San
Nicholas* surrendered to Nelson; the next moment, hearing

shots from the *San Josef*, Nelson ordered his boarders who were already on the *San Nicholas* to board the other, which was alongside. This was achieved without loss on either side, for by this time the *San Josef* had already surrendered to Sir William. As the senior naval captain present, however, Nelson received the swords of the two Spanish captains and their surviving officers.

Nelson's courage and initiative in breaking from the line and giving battle to both groups simultaneously was at once recognised by Sir John Jervis, who wrote a personal letter to the Admiralty praising his subordinate's action. He did not, however, mention Nelson's name in his official report of the action which was published in the *London Gazette*. To remedy this omission a detailed account of the battle pointing out that Sir John's manoeuvre would have failed but for Captain Nelson's initiative, and which gave a graphic description of the boarding of the *San Nicholas*, and then the use of the captured ship as a bridge from which to board and capture yet another Spanish 'first rater', appeared in all the papers under the heading of 'Nelson's patent Bridge for Boarding First Raters'. This was written by Nelson himself, and sent to his friend Captain William Locker, RN, in England, with the request that he copy it out and send it to all the newspapers, though emphatically not under Nelson's name. Another version of the battle was written by a Colonel Drinkwater, who had seen the battle at a distance from one of Sir John's scouting frigates. Drinkwater later recorded that the morning after the battle he was visited by Nelson, who insisted on giving him an account of the battle before he reported to Sir John Jervis on his flagship. Possibly Nelson's object in doing this was to insure himself, by establishing his version of events in the public's eye, against any disciplinary action Jervis might decide to take against him for leaving the line. That is the charitable view. However, it seems much more likely that ambition was the driving force behind these various manoeuvres.

England and her Navy needed a hero, and Nelson was promptly promoted to Rear-Admiral and made a Knight of the Bath. He could well have enjoyed a baronetcy, but at the same time as he sent his own version of events back to England he also sent a letter asking friends to drop the hint that he could not afford to sustain the expense of hereditary honours.

Nevertheless, he directed the College of Heralds that he wished his coat-of-arms to show the British lion trampling on the flag of Spain, and that his crest was to be the outline of the *San Josef.* The Battle of St Vincent showed the world not only his immense courage and seamanship, but also those streaks of vanity, ambition and ruthlessness in his character which, if he had not died at Trafalgar, would certainly have brought to him the same degree of disrespect and disdain which he eventually brought to Emma and Sir William.

The news of their victory gave fresh heart to the beleaguered Court at Naples, and Nelson's letters to Sir William were avidly listened to when Emma read them to the Royal Family. It was a bright moment which was not to last. Sir William was feeling ill again, writing to his friend Sir Joseph Banks that 'the constant agitation and fatigue of mind which I have undergone for six years past has injured myself very much, and my stomach and bilious complaints are more severe and frequent.' He wrote to Greville in a similar vein, throwing out heavy hints that he hoped the King would soon grant him leave, or even perhaps allow him to retire, though he did not wish to resign until he knew what rewards the government might have in store for him. The only reward Sir William wanted was money, preferably a grant or a substantial pension. His expenses on entertainment had been heavy, and he had also managed to spend considerably more on vases and pictures as Napoleon systematically dismembered Italy.

The next news Sir William heard of Nelson was sobering. The newly fashionable hero had been placed in command of an expedition against Tenerife. It had been a miserable fiasco, with heavy casualties, and Nelson himself had been shot in the elbow as he stepped into the assault boat. His stepson had staunched the flow of blood, and as soon as he was back aboard his ship his right arm had had to be amputated at the elbow. The operation was not wholly successful and he was evacuated to England to recover.

When the news of Tenerife and of Nelson's injury reached Italy, it was greeted with mixed feelings. The French at Toulon must have heaved a sigh of relief, because during the blockade prior to the British evacuation of the Mediterranean, Nelson had been the scourge of the merchants and their ships who had tried to trade with France. The French themselves had enormous respect for his seamanship and the fighting abilities of his men. Sir William, on the other hand, was reduced to the depths of depression, a depression which was compounded when at the same time French pressure on King Ferdinand forced him to displace Acton as his Prime Minister and appoint in his place the Marquis di Gallo. The Marquis was, in Emma's words, 'a frivolous ignorant self-conceited coxcomb, that thinks of nothing but his fine embroidered coat, ring and snuff box'. However, he disliked the English and admired the French. The Court was now thrown into further confusion, as while the King and the Marquis were the overt government, the Queen and Acton were still the major powers behind the scenes, and they wove the Hamiltons into an even tighter web of intrigue. Sir William could no longer think of leave, or of a graceful retirement with a large pension. He now began to worry about how he could capitalise on his latest collection of vases, and how to pack up his pictures and send them safely home, before the French were at the gates of Naples and he lost the lot.

The Christmas of 1797 was a miserable one. Prince Augustus, unable to resist the lure of Naples, returned to plague Hamilton's patience and his pocket. Then came news of sinister French preparations at Toulon; thirty thousand troops were quartered on the city, and a hundred troopships—some reports said three hundred—were fitting out in the harbour, escorted by the French battle fleet commanded by Admiral de Brueys. The nearest British naval force was still blockading Cadiz, and Britain's prime strategic worry was to prevent the French and Spanish fleets from joining. Most worrying of all was the destination of the invasion army that Napoleon was preparing. Both the Neapolitans and the Earl St Vincent— as Sir John Jervis had now become—believed that the French expedition was directed against Naples. With the Marquis di Gallo's hand on the helm of Neapolitan foreign policy, Naples could not ask the English for assistance; Sir William, now nearing seventy, seemed despondent and content to let matters take their inevitable course. The fact was that Sir William, who belonged to a different age, could not adjust to the new warfare. He neither understood nor cared what the war was all about, or even why the French seemed so successful everywhere. All Sir William could understand was that one was either a Briton or a Frenchman, and that it was his duty to behave as the former. But he was now dreaming of home, of the society of the *cognoscenti* he had once known, and he engaged himself in writing prolix letters to European monarchs whom he believed would purchase his vases, oblivious to the fact that France controlled all the lines of communication north of Naples.

The Queen, Acton and Emma took matters into their own hands. On 7 April 1798 a privateer was hired at the Queen's expense to take an up-to-date summary of the situation to the Earl St Vincent, together with an appeal for a British fleet to come to the relief of the city. Hamilton seemed totally unaware of what was going on, reporting to London a week later that the Court 'flattered themselves that a British fleet is actually—which I must doubt—on its way to Naples'.

Two days after Sir William wrote these somewhat cynical words, despatches arrived confirming that a British fleet was indeed on its way. The reasons for the decision were simple. St Vincent, realising that whether or not Naples was in danger, sooner or later the French fleet would have to be brought to battle, decided to try to catch it outside Toulon before it could set sail into the

Mediterranean and bring havoc to its chosen destination. In this resolve he anticipated the English Prime Minister Pitt's decision. Pitt had heard reports—accurate ones as they later proved to be—that Napoleon was taking his army to Egypt, where after conquering the Egyptians he planned to cut a canal through the Isthmus of Suez and take his fleet and army to India. Pitt decided that Britain's presence was needed in the Mediterranean, first to support the few remaining anti-French states left; but second, and more important, he realised that if he could find and destroy the French fleet, this would leave the Royal Navy sitting astride the French lines of communication. Pitt decided to place Nelson in command of a squadron and charge it with the task of destroying the French fleet. On this, though unknown to each other, Pitt and St Vincent were in complete agreement. Nelson was recalled from leave, pronounced fit to serve, and despatched with the *Vanguard* to report to St Vincent at the mouth of the Tagus. Nelson himself had no idea what his assignment would be but assumed his orders were to continue the Spanish blockade. On reaching the Tagus, St Vincent opened Nelson's orders from Pitt to find that they coincided with his own plans. As yet the Admiral did not have a squadron for Nelson, but he sent him with a small force of fast ships to reconnoitre the Port of Toulon and to remain in that general area until St Vincent was able to send him reinforcements. Nelson's other instructions were to find out what help Naples and the other smaller ports in the Mediterranean could offer the British fleet in the way of supplies, intelligence and, if possible, the loan of frigates to act as scouts and support for the main English fleet when it arrived.

Nelson left Cadiz on 2 May, but within three weeks he was seeking shelter off Sardinia, his fleet scattered in a violent storm which had dismasted the *Vanguard*. Over-confidence had been his crime, and in a letter to his wife he was man enough to admit it.

Vanguard, Island of St Peter's
in Sardinia
24 May 1798

'My dearest Fanny,—I ought not to call what has happened to the *Vanguard* by the cold name of accident, I believe firmly that it was the Almighty's goodness to check my consummate vanity. I hope it has made me a better officer, as I feel confident it has made me a better man. I kiss with all humility the rod. Figure to yourself a vain man on Sunday evening at sunset walking in his cabin with a squadron about him who looked up to their chief to lead them to glory and in whom this chief placed the firmest reliance that the proudest ships in equal numbers belonging to France would have bowed their flags, and with a very rich prize lying by him. Figure to yourself this proud conceited man, when the sun rose on Monday morning, his ship dismasted, his fleet dispersed and himself in such distress that the meanest frigate out of France would have been a very unwelcome guest. But it has pleased Almighty God to bring us into a safe port, where altho' we are refused the rights of humanity, yet the *Vanguard* will in two days get to sea again as an English man-of-war. If the ship had been in England months would have been taken to send her to sea. Here my operations will not be delayed four days, and I shall join the rest of my fleet on the rendezvous. If this letter gets to you be so good as to write a line to Lord Spencer telling him that the *Vanguard* is fitted tolerably for sea, and that what has happened will not retard my operations.

I have wrote to Lord Spencer by another but I still wish you to write a line to say we are all well for yours may arrive and his Lordship's miscarry.

Vanguard's damages:

Foremast	⎱	gone
Foretopmast	⎰	overboard

Foretopgallant mast and all the yards
    forward
Bowsprit sprung in three places
Maintopmast and topgallantmast with all the yards
    except topgallant yard and rigging—gone overboard

Mizentopmast, topgallant mast and all the yards
   belonging to topgallant yard—gone overboard
A topsail yard washed out
The mainchains, starboard quarters gallery
   washed away with one boat and a bower anchor
Mr Thomas Meek (who was recommended by Mr
Hussy, my brother, Suckling, etc) killed and several
seamen hurt.

To Lady Nelson, Round Wood, Ipswich.'

When Nelson eventually arrived at Toulon, he found
that the French armada had already sailed and he
returned to his rendezvous, where on 7 June he was
joined by the ten ships of the line which St Vincent had
sent him. His new orders were to 'take, sink, burn and
destroy the enemy fleet'.

Nelson now had his battleships, but his frigates—the
eyes and ears of his fleet—had been scattered in the
storm which had dismasted the *Vanguard*. He needed
three things: first, frigates; second, accurate intelligence
on the whereabouts of the French fleet; and third,
confirmation that he could be revictualled and watered at
any Neapolitan port he might call into either on the
mainland or in Sicily. On 14 June he hove to within sight
of Naples and sent Captain Troubridge ashore in the
Mutine.

The King and Sir William were in a quandary.
Technically Naples was still neutral, and the French
were only sixty miles away. Napoleon, honouring his
treaty with the King of Spain, had assured Ferdinand
that he would leave his Kingdom alone as long as it did
not take sides, and to make sure the bargain was kept he
had replaced the unpleasant Monsieur Mackau, his
Ambassador, by an even more sinister figure, Monsieur
Garat, who had personally read the death sentence to
Louis XVI. The King could not and dare not supply
frigates or open his ports to Nelson. Emma went to the
Queen, and Sir John Acton, taking his life in his hands,
gave Troubridge a written undertaking that the ports

would be open to the British, and that either he or the Queen would inform the relevant port officials 'under the rose' to be as helpful as possible. All Sir William was able to tell Nelson was that the French had taken Malta. Emma wrote Nelson her best wishes, and sent him a personal note from the Queen bidding God speed. Troubridge left Naples two hours after he had landed and Nelson disappeared on his long chase after the French fleet. He searched the Mediterranean from Naples to Alexandria without finding them, for unknown to him, though he was sailing the same route, he was slightly ahead of them. Five weeks later he was back in the Neapolitan port of Syracuse, provisioning for the first time in two months. The Port Commandant showed him every courtesy, his ships were replenished with food and water, and his every need was attended to. Once the revictualling was completed, he sailed again for Alexandria.

There has been considerable controversy over this revictualling, which both Nelson and Emma later claimed was due to Emma's intercession with the Queen, and the orders given 'under the rose'. Emma's part in this operation has been denied her by most historians, on the grounds that Nelson's formal letters to St Vincent and Sir William complained of the lack of assistance and the anti-British attitude of the Port Commandant. But it can be assumed that these letters were written by a Nelson who fully expected his letters to be intercepted by the French, or at least read by pro-French members of the Neapolitan administration or captured by the Spaniards on their way to St Vincent at Gibraltar. His own notebook, which he cannot have thought would be captured by the enemy or read by spies, contains a copy of a note to Sir William and Emma dated the evening he left Syracuse which reads: 'My dear friends, thanks for your exertions we have victualled and watered, and surely watering at the fountain of Arethusa [a classical reference to Syracuse] we must have victory. We shall sail with the first breeze, and be assured I shall

Emma Hamilton in 1794. From a painting by Frederick Rehburg.
(National Maritime Museum, Greenwich).

Emma at eighteen: two paintings by George Romney. (Left: National Portrait Gallery. Right: National Maritime Museum.)

Uppark, the seat of Sir Harry Featherstonehaugh. From an engraving.
(Portsmouth City Museum).

Charles Towneley in his study with Charles Greville (left),
d'Hancarville and Thomas Astle, by John Zoffany.
(Towneley Hall Art Gallery Museums,
Burnley Borough Council).

Sir William Hamilton, 1777. Studio of Sir Joshua Reynolds.
(National Portrait Gallery).

Two portraits of Nelson c. 1800. Left: by W. Beechey. Right: The only known portrait in civilian clothes, by H. Füger. (National Portrait Gallery).

Nelson by an unknown Neapolitan artist.

(This and the following five illustrations are miniatures from the
Nelson-Ward Collection in the Royal Naval Museum, Portsmouth
and are reproduced by permission of the Museum. The items in the
collection all belonged to Horatia Nelson and were presented to the
Museum by her descendants.)

Sir William Hamilton by an unknown Neapolitan artist.

Emma Hamilton by Bone after a portrait by Madame le Brun. Sir William left it to Nelson in his will with these words:

The copy of Madame le Brun's picture of Emma, in enamel, by Bone, I give to my dearest friend Lord Nelson, Duke of Bronte; a very small token of the great regard I have for his Lordship, the most virtuous, loyal, and truly brave character I ever met with. God bless him, and shame fall on those who do not say 'Amen'.

*Emma's mother, Mrs Cadogan, by an unknown
Neapolitan artist.*

The King and Queen of Naples, by an unknown
Neapolitan artist.

Above: Prince Bomba, eldest son of the King and Queen of Naples.
Below: Two other children of the King and Queen of Naples.

Merton Place, Surrey, by E. Locker Hawke. (National Maritime Museum).

Two sketches of life at Merton, by George Baxter:
Above: Horatia Nelson standing on a chair.
Below: Lady Hamilton and friends playing cards.
(National Maritime Museum).

Emma and Nelson: a pair of miniatures by J.H. Schmidt, 1800. That of Emma is inscribed in her handwriting on the back, 'This portrait of Emma Hamilton was in all the battles with the virtuous gallant and heroic Nelson. He called it his "Guardian Angel" and thought he could not be victorious if he could not see it in the midst of battle'. (National Maritime Museum).

Mourning locket commemorating the death of Nelson, which belonged to Emma Hamilton. (Nelson–Ward Collection, Royal Naval Museum, Portsmouth).

return . . .'

Neither Emma nor Sir William shared his hopes though Emma prayed for him. She also wrote to him, sending the letter by one of Nelson's missing frigates which had belatedly arrived off Naples. After giving him the news of the appointment of Garat, she added: 'I am afraid all is lost here and I am grieved to the heart for our dear charming Queen who deserves a better fate. I write to you my dear sir in confidence and in a hurry. I hope you will not quit the Mediterranean without taking *us*. We have our leave, and everything ready at a day's notice to go, but yet I trust in God and you that we shall destroy these monsters before we go from hence, surely their reign cannot last long. If you have any opportunity write to us . . . you do not know how your letters comfort us.'

Emma may well have been worrying privately, but she made a point of never appearing in public without wearing either a sash or a ribbon in her hat embroidered in gold with 'God Prosper Nelson'. It was a neat gesture, calculated to irritate Garat, who anyway shortly afterwards left for Rome. Sir William made some half-hearted suggestions to Acton that the Neapolitans mount a pre-emptive war against the French army in Rome, but his plan was not well thought out. The suggestion did however start secret negotiations with Maria Carolina's Austrian relations to see if they would support such a reckless adventure; otherwise he devoted most of his time to attending to his collections and their possible sale or shipment home. While Emma attended to his official paperwork, the worried and weakened Sir William—plagued by bilious attacks and diarrhoea— compiled an inventory of his pictures. He dated it as having been commenced on 14 July 1798 and it lists 347 items, including works by Rubens, Rembrandt, Veronese, Van Dyck, at least sixteen by Canaletto, and seven by Titian. No fewer than fourteen were versions of Emma in various poses: three each by Romney and Tischbein, two each by Vigée Lebrun and Gavin

Hamilton, while Sir Joshua Reynolds, Angelica Kauff-mann, a Mr Head and an unknown artist were all represented by one apiece. There were also at least eighteen separate versions of Vesuvius in eruption, many by Hamilton's *protégé* and illustrator Pietro Fabris. Hardly a famous painter was not represented. Although occasionally Sir William's attributions have been faulted—for example his Leonardo da Vinci's *Head of a Laughing Boy* is now generally accepted as being by Bernardino Luini—the collection represented a stunning cross-section of the whole field of classical and the then leading contemporary artists. There are certain clues as to how Sir William obtained several of the paintings. Two fine Giordanos, and another pair by his pupil Simonelli, came from a Carmelite church in Naples; Hamilton's note reads: 'Where I left copies by Candido in their place.' Candido was an illustrator whom Hamilton also commissioned to make water-colour copies of the wall-paintings at Pompeii. As to quality, one picture which Hamilton described briefly as a *Portrait of a Moresco Slave* by Velázquez, fetched £1,240,000 when it was auctioned at Christie's in 1972.

It must have been a gloomy task, as throughout that bright Neapolitan August the pictures were packed and crated up. Soon the Palazzo Sessa was bare of the treasures which had adorned it for so long. The vases were also packed. Hamilton had offered them to the King of Prussia for £7,000, but the King had not taken up the offer, reckoning quite correctly that the French would be in Naples before Hamilton would be able to send them to him. What nobody in Naples—or Europe for that matter—knew at the time was that shortly after lunch on 15 August, Nelson's squadron sighted the French fleet at anchor off Alexandria. Nelson decided to attack that same evening, and he announced to his captains who were dining aboard the flagship: 'Before this time tomorrow, I shall have gained a Peerage or Westminster Abbey.'

VI

September–December 1798

Victory and Retreat

'If I was the King of England I would
make you the most noble puissant
Duke Nelson, Marquis Nile, Earl
Alexandria, Viscount Pyramid,
Baron Crocodile and Prince
Victory so that posterity might
have you in all forms.'

Emma, Lady Hamilton to
Baron Nelson of the Nile

The French fleet was lying at anchor off Alexandria. Its commander, Admiral François de Brueys, had been unable to find a pilot to navigate his great ships through the tortuous channels that wound round the shoals and into the harbour and had therefore adopted a position which he believed was almost impregnable, drawing up his line of battle so that the fleet was moored in a convex line running parallel to the shores of Aboukir Bay. Between his line and the shore were the shoals, inside which no ship was believed capable of manoeuvre, and on the shore itself were the French army's artillery batteries to give him covering fire should he decide to make sail and head out to sea. To strengthen his position still further, he had ordered all the guns on the port or landward side of each ship to be transferred across to the seaward side, thereby doubling the strength of his broadsides. To keep an even keel, the spaces left by the missing guns were filled with cannonballs and stores.

De Brueys had thirteen battleships and four frigates, and a total complement of 1,196 guns pointed menacingly towards the oncoming British fleet. Nelson had the same number of battleships, but no frigates. He had only slightly fewer guns, but his were ranged down both sides of his ships, so that at any one time he would have less than half the firepower of the French. The wind blew evenly from the north-west, towards the shore, giving Nelson the advantage of manoeuvrability. The French, unable to cope with the on-shore wind, had furled their sails and were anchored by the bow. Nelson calculated that he would reach the French fleet just as the sun was setting, and his plan was for his fleet to operate in pairs, two of his ships to take on one French, in this way working slowly down their line. This would increase his firepower, and when it came to boarding it would double his manpower. As he was converging with the French fleet bow on, he gave orders that each English ship should be prepared to anchor by the stern as it drew level with its French counterpart.

This was to ensure that it stopped in the correct position, as to drop a bow anchor would have meant sailing over it, thereby dragging it out again. His last signal was for 'close action', which meant that he believed his best chances lay in getting aboard the French, as with their superior firepower he had no wish for an artillery duel. It was a sound and sensible plan, but one which all aboard realised was going to be a very costly one when it came to counting the casualties. Nevertheless it was without doubt the best that could have been devised in the then known circumstances. However, the course of the battle was to take a sudden, a dramatic, and for Nelson a most fortunate course.

The British line was led by Captain Hood in the *Zealous*, closely followed by Captain Foley in the *Goliath*. Foley had the faster ship, and, perhaps by accident but probably by design, he overtook Hood, becoming the leading ship. Foley had a French atlas on board which showed that there was just enough depth to sail between the French line and the shore. He also reasoned that if the French were anchored by the bow, there would surely be depth enough for them to swing at their anchors. Nelson had asked for close action so Foley, in a brilliant piece of initiative, ducked inside the line and at point-blank range fired his first broadside into the unarmed and unprotected inside flank of the French. Foley was followed by the next three British ships, and the four of them sailed closely down the French line, demolishing them one by one with their broadsides. There was no need to board, it was just slaughter.

The fifth in the line, Captain Troubridge in the *Culloden*, went aground as he tried to follow Foley, and Nelson who came next in the *Vanguard* launched his attack on de Brueys' flagship *L'Orient*, which mounted a broadside of 120 guns to his 37. With six sets of colours flying in case any were shot away, he anchored by the stern on the seaward side of de Brueys. Foley's tactic had already accounted for four of the French ships, and Nelson was now joined in his determined attack by four more of his fleet, so that as well as the *Vanguard* the *Orient* was fighting the *Minotaur*, the *Bellerophon*, the *Defence* and the *Majestic* on her seaward side, as well as taking a battering from the *Zealous* and another of Foley's followers, the *Alexander*.

After two hours of almost continuous firing, the *Orient* was still fighting, but eight of the French had already surrendered and the remainder knew they were doomed. As news of the eighth surrender was signalled to Nelson, he was struck in the head by a stray shot and collapsed on the quarterdeck, crying out, 'I am killed; remember me to my wife.' He was quickly carried down to the surgeons, who equally quickly discovered that in fact he had a minor scalp wound and that he was in no danger. What had happened was that a fragment of shot had cut into his forehead and a flap of skin had fallen down over his one good eye, effectively blinding him. Three stitches and ten minutes later, all that was left was a blinding headache. Nelson stayed below, feverishly trying to compose an account of the battle which still raged above.

The *Orient* was now in her last throes. Every mast and

shroud had been shot away; most of her crew had been killed or wounded. The British fire still poured into her, to be answered only occasionally as some French gunner despairingly managed to load and fire his gun. On the *Vanguard* itself the casualties had been enormous. Three times her gun crews had been wiped out, each time being replaced by substitutes while the dead were thrown overboard. But the *Vanguard* was still a fighting ship while the *Orient* was little more than a hulk. Clearly silhouetted against the glow of the battle was the *Orient*'s captain, Admiral de Brueys. He was mortally wounded, and had had himself lashed to a chair on the quarterdeck. Beside him stood a nine-year-old boy, his godson Alexis, who was the son of the commodore of the flagship *M. Casa-Bianca.* The boy was dressed in a miniature officer's uniform, and tied to his hat were the colours of the Republic. Suddenly the word spread around the surrounding English ships: The *Orient* was on fire.

Within minutes she was blazing from stem to stern but de Brueys, high up on the quarterdeck, was far above the blaze. One of his own cannons exploded, and a sliver of white hot metal neatly amputated both his legs. Still the boy stayed beside him, while those who survived among her crew leapt into the sea. Now there was a lull in the firing as the English ships desperately tried to drag themselves away before they too were engulfed in the flames. The *Vanguard* was warped clear, her hands desperately working the anchor windlass, though the *Alexander*'s sails caught fire from the sparks of the dying *Orient*. The sudden lull in the firing, coupled with the frenzied activity as the *Vanguard* tried to pull away from the inferno, brought Nelson up on to the deck again, just in time to see the terrifying tableau of de Brueys and his young godson outlined against the flames when suddenly the *Orient* exploded. The flagship blew apart with an appalling flash, and for some minutes the only sounds were the clatter and the splashes of fragments falling either on to the decks of the British fleet or into the water. A silver spoon from de Brueys' dinner service landed on the poop of the *Bellerophon*—probably the largest and most valuable piece to be recovered. Nelson immediately ordered away his one remaining serviceable lifeboat to pick up survivors and to search for de Brueys and the child. Some seventy French sailors were picked up but there was no trace of the brave if incongruous couple from the *Orient*'s quarterdeck.* The light thrown out by the explosion clearly illuminated the last stages of the battle. After a short lull, the firing started again but there was little more to be done. By dawn it was all over. Eleven of the thirteen French battleships had either surrendered or been sunk. Two escaped into the darkness.

Of the four frigates, one was sunk, two escaped, and the fourth blew herself up rather than surrender. Four thousand Frenchmen were killed while the British total of killed and wounded was less than eight hundred; not a single ship had been lost. Napoleon's army was now stranded in Egypt and, as William Pitt had planned and prayed, the British navy was now unopposed in the Mediterranean and had a stranglehold on the French lines of communication and supply.

Assured of all the honours that he had ever desired, Nelson went below to write his victory despatch. It began as had Rodney's, almost a hundred years before: 'Almighty God, having blessed His Majesty's arms with victory. . .' The despatch certainly gave the Almighty most of the credit, but characteristically it omitted to mention either Captain Foley or the tactic he had been inspired to take and which had been the major contribution to the victory.

Whilst Nelson in the battered *Vanguard* limped slowly back to Naples to refit, two of his faster ships brought news of the victory to Naples and Gibraltar. The *Mutine*, a small speedy brig, arrived in Naples on Monday 1 September and gave Sir William Hamilton the news. Naples, the Queen and Emma were swept up in a wave of

---

*Today the child is remembered only in the contemporary poem which the scene inspired commencing, 'The boy stood on the burning deck whence all but he had fled'. The words are familiar, but their context has long been forgotten.

happiness and relief. Contemporary letters give the best description, and Emma's wordy note to Nelson written over several days as was her habit, should come first.

8 September 1798 Naples

'My dear, dear Sir,

How shall I begin, what shall I say to you? It is impossible I can write, for since last Monday I am delirious with joy, and assure you I have a fever caused by agitation and pleasure. God, what a victory! Never, never has there been anything half so glorious, so compleat. I fainted when I heard the joyful news, and fell on my side and am hurt, but well of that. I should feel it a glory to die in such a cause. No, I would not like to die until I see and embrace the Victor of the Nile. How shall I describe to you the transports of Maria Carolina, it is not possible. She fainted and kissed her husband, her children, walked about the room, cried, kissed, and embraced every person near her, exclaiming, "Oh, brave Nelson, oh, God bless and protect our brave deliverer, oh, Nelson, Nelson, what do we not owe to you, oh Victor, Saviour of Italy, oh, that my swollen heart could now tell him personally what we owe to him!"

You may judge, my dear Sir, of the rest, but my head will not permit me to tell you half the rejoicing. The Neapolitans are mad with joy, and if you were here now, you would be killed with kindness. Sonnets on sonnets, illuminations, rejoicings; not a French dog dare show his face. How I glory in the honour of my Country and my Countryman! I walk and tread in the air with pride, feeling I was born in the same land with the victor Nelson and his gallant band. But no more, I cannot, dare not, trust myself, for I am not well.

I send you two letters from my adorable Queen. One was written to me the day we received the glorious news, the other yesterday. Keep them, as they are in her own handwriting. I have kept copies only, but I feel that you ought to have them. If you had seen our meeting after the battle, but I will keep it all for your arrival. I could not do justice to her feeling nor to my own, with writing it; and we are preparing your apartment against you come. I hope it will not be long, for Sir William and I are so impatient to embrace you. I wish you could have seen our house the three nights of illumination. It was covered with your glorious name. There were three thousand lamps, and there should have been three million if we had had time. All the English vie with each other in celebrating this most gallant and ever-memorable victory. Sir William is ten years younger since the happy news, and he now only wishes to see his friend to be completely happy. How he glories in you when your name is mentioned. He cannot contain his joy. For God's sake come to Naples soon. We receive so many sonnets and letters of congratulations. I sent you some of them to show you how much your success is felt here. How I felt for poor Troubridge. He must have been so angry on the sandbank, so brave an officer! In short I pity those who were not in the battle. I would have been rather an English powdermonkey, or a swab in that great victory, than an emperor out of it, but you will be so tired of all this. Write or come soon to Naples, and rejoin your ever sincere and obliged friend,

Emma Hamilton

P.S. The Queen at this moment sent a diamond ring to Captain Hoste (who had brought the news of the victory), six butts of wine (two casks, for the officers), and for every man on board a guinea each. Her letter is in English and comes as from an unknown person, but a well-wisher to our country, and an admirer of our gallant Nelson. As war is not yet declared with France, she could not show herself so openly as she wished, but she has done so much, and rejoiced so very publicly, that all the world sees it. She bids me to say that she longs more to see you than any woman with child can long for anything she may take a fancy to, and she shall be forever unhappy if you do not come. God bless you my dear, dear friend.

My dress from head to foot is all Nelson... Even my

shawl is in blue with gold anchors all over. My earrings are Nelson's anchors; in short, we are be-Nelsoned all over. I send you some sonnets, but I must have taken a ship on purpose to send you all written on you. Once more, God bless you. My mother desires her love to you. I am so sorry to write in such a hurry. I am afraid you will not be able to read this scrawl.'

The *Vanguard* ended her passage to Naples at the end of a tow rope, but even that lent a romantic aura to the occasion. By either luck or design it happened to be the anniversary of Ferdinand's coronation, and Nelson and his victorious crews were made much of. The English authoress Miss Cornelia Knight who was a house guest of the Hamiltons described the arrival in her diary.

'In the evening, went out with Sir William and Lady Hamilton, music etc, to meet Admiral Nelson, who in the *Vanguard*, with the *Thalia* frigate (Captain Newhouse), was seen coming in. We went on board, about a league out at sea, and sailed with him: soon after us, the King came on board, and stayed till the anchor was dropped. He embraced the Admiral with the greatest warmth, and said he wished he could have been in the engagement, and served under his orders; and that he likewise wished he could have been in England when the news of the victory arrived there. He went down to see the ship, and was delighted to perceive the care taken of a wounded man, who had two to serve him, and one reading to him. He asked to see the hat which saved the Admiral's life, when he was wounded in the head with a splinter. The Queen was taken with a fit of ague when she was coming on board with the Princesses. Commodore Caracciollo came soon after the King, and many of the Neapolitan nobility, bands of music, etc. It happened to be the anniversary of our King's coronation. The Admiral came on shore with us, and said it was the first time he had been out of his ship for six months, except once on board the *Lord St Vincent*. [*sic*] The Russian ambassador and all the Legation came out to meet him. When we landed at the Health Office, the applauses and the crowd of people were beyond description. Admiral Nelson is little, and not remarkable in his person in either way; but he has great animation of countenance, and activity in his appearance: his manners are unaffectedly simple and modest. He lodges at Sir William Hamilton's who has given him the upper apartment. The whole city is mad with joy...'

Nelson was taken ashore, and Emma bathed the wound on his head which was still giving him considerable pain. Within three days, he was able to write to his wife Fanny, who was still living quietly near Ipswich:

'I hope one day to have the pleasure of introducing you to Lady Hamilton,. She is one of the very best women in this world. How few could have made the turn she has. She is an honour to her sex and a proof that even reputation may be regained, but I own it requires a great soul. Her kindness with Sir William to me is more than I can express. I am in their house, and I may tell you it required all the kindness of my friends to set me up. I believe Lady Hamilton intends writing you.'

What Nelson did not tell his wife was that he was physically and emotionally exhausted. The long search for the French fleet had taken a heavy toll of his nerves and Nelson, always prone to insecurity and doubly tried by the loneliness of command, had already been on the verge of breakdown when the French fleet had been sighted. The battle and his ensuing victory had drained whatever strength he had left in him, and the seven-week voyage back to Naples had not helped him to recover his peace of mind. He had written a brief note to Hamilton saying that for four years and nine months he had had hardly a moment's rest and that he felt 'as if a girth were buckled taut over my breast, and I endeavour in the night to get it loose'. This was perhaps an exaggeration, but there is no doubt that a monumental depression settled on him in the wake of his triumph. At times he felt ready to die, writing to St Vincent that, 'I never expect my dear Lord, to see your face again. May it please God that this is the finish to that fever of anxiety which I have endured from the middle of June.'

The Hamiltons' invitation was doubly welcome. At last he could rest and Sir William, who seemed totally rejuvenated by the turn of events, took much of the administrative load off his shoulders. His ships were sent to the Royal dockyards to be repaired, and though he was continuously fêted in Naples there was also time for rest and tranquillity. He was secure in his triumph, and though the festivities in his honour were perhaps a drain on his energies, at least they lacked the burden of responsibility. Exhausted but content that his mission was successfully accomplished, Nelson allowed himself to be carried along by events. The Neapolitan Court never needed any excuse for a party; now there were plenty. A British fleet was moored in the bay, Nelson was their honoured and pampered guest, and the spectre of Bonaparte had receded into the sands of Egypt. Banquet followed banquet; galas, spectacles and firework displays occupied every evening as the Court wallowed in its gaiety.

At first the whole business irritated Nelson, who complained of feeling unwell, and he described his Italian hosts as 'a country of fiddlers and poets, whores and scoundrels'. When he wrote these words, however, he was probably suffering from a hangover, as on the previous night there had been a monumental party in honour of his fortieth birthday. The Palazzo Sessa had been decorated with trophies of the battle; eight hundred had taken supper and Sir William had invited a further seventeen hundred for the dancing. In the midst of all this, his stepson Josiah had become disgustingly drunk, and had to be taken out by two of his brother officers. Legend has it that the cause of this outburst was the attention that Nelson was showing Emma, and that is certainly what Josiah spread around afterwards as an excuse for his behaviour, claiming that Nelson was insulting his mother. Judging from contemporary Neapolitan accounts this is a half-truth. Emma, who had shown young Josiah the town during their previous visit when he was merely a boy, did not regard him as sufficiently interesting or distinguished to sit at the top table at dinner and could not find space for him on her dance card. Unwittingly she had snubbed him, and it was sheer jealousy on the part of Josiah, an uncouth and foul-mouthed young man, that prompted him to spread these rumours.

Josiah was already in disgrace. He had not been present at the battle, and St Vincent had recently written to Nelson that 'it would be a breach of friendship to conceal from you that he loves drink and low company, is thoroughly ignorant of all forms of service, inattentive, obstinate and wrongheaded beyond measure.' St Vincent went on to tell Nelson equally bluntly that if Josiah had not been his stepson he would have kicked him out of the Navy months ago.

It must have been galling to Josiah to see his stepfather, with whom he had a love-hate relationship, at the pinnacle of his success while he was in disgrace. From now on, Josiah was to become the source of many of the more scurrilous tales that began to permeate the fleet and that inevitably soon found their way back to England.

Emma rather shared Nelson's opinion on Neapolitan society. During the party she had danced with Captain Ball, one of his closest friends, and had murmured to him as they passed a group of Neapolitan courtiers and their ladies that 'there was not a woman there who wasn't a whore, nor a man who didn't deserve the gallows.' Ball had promptly passed her remark on to Nelson, with the added compliment that it was pleasant to have a hostess who understood 'we simple sailors'.

Emma's earthiness may well have been the first thing that appealed to Nelson. Their backgrounds were not dissimilar, at least to the extent that in the glittering salons of Naples they were probably the only two who came from humble families. Nelson's family were minor clergymen, or else engaged in trade in a small way in Norfolk. He never mentioned the fact in polite company, but one brother-in-law was a carter, and an elder brother, a clerk at the Admiralty, was living in sin in a London suburb and was not above fiddling his books. Nelson talked almost as 'country' as Emma, except that his was a slow Norfolk drawl. However at this time, apart from being grateful to Emma for bathing his head, Nelson had no further desire than to finish his job and get home to England and to his wife and the glory that he knew awaited him. He was also conscious that if he stayed in such surroundings, his head would be turned, for he was aware of his vanity. In the same Messianic strain that he used for his despatches to London, he wrote to his father, 'Almighty God has made me an instrument of human happiness ... all my caution will be necessary to prevent vanity from showing itself superior to my gratitude.'

Nelson's victory revived the negotiations which Maria Carolina had been conducting with the Austrians for a pre-emptive march on Rome to drive out the French. Austria now agreed to supply a general and the King began raising an army of 45,000 men. Nelson heartily approved of the plan and he and Hamilton pressed the Court to mount the expedition and the King to lead it personally. While these preparations were in hand, Nelson sailed off to Malta to check on the French occupation of the island. He found it strongly held, and leaving Captain Ball to blockade it, returned to Naples. This short expedition—he was away just under three weeks—made him ill again. He was coughing and suffering from blinding headaches. His stump, or fin as he called it, was giving him continuous pain, and he had a series of slight convulsions. Epilepsy apart, he was on the verge of a total mental and physical breakdown. Immediately on landing, he gratefully accepted the hospitality of the Hamiltons, and went to bed.

Emma nursed him, bathed him in asses' milk, soothed his eye and, probably most important, kept him quiet. She ran his errands, wrote letters at his dictation, and took his messages to the Court and to the Queen. In fact she was indispensable. She was also someone he could talk to; someone who had no pomp, who like him had lived her life on her nerves and on the borderline of insecurity. She tried to help him with Josiah as well, teaching him manners and going out of her way to soothe him by offering to teach him to dance. Josiah appeared grateful, and was so altered that Nelson was to write to his wife that he was greatly improved and that 'I am sure he likes Lady Hamilton more than any other female. She would fashion him in six months in spite of himself.' Josiah's apparent co-operation however was a façade, for he reported back to his mother that he hated not only the Hamiltons but dancing as well. Despite their proximity, and the numerous delights of Naples, there was still no affair. Nor did Emma want one. A note she scribbled to Nelson has survived, in which she makes a play on the motto of the Order of the Knights of the Bath, of which both Sir William and Nelson were members. It was a note written specifically to lift his depression:

'May you live long long long for the sake of your country, your King, your family, all Europe, Asia, Africa and America ... but particularly for Sir William and myself ... I told Her Majesty we only wanted Lady Nelson to be the female 'Tria Juncta in Uno', for we all love you, and yet all three differently and yet all equally—if you can make this out. Sir William laughs at us, but he owns women have great souls, at least his has. I would not be a lukewarm friend for the world—I am no one's enemy, and unfortunately am difficult and cannot make friendship with all.'

Here is Emma telling Nelson that the Queen loved him out of gratitude, his wife as she ought ... and herself? Well, she loved him as someone to cherish and look after; with whom she had an instant *rapport* and in whom she could confide. Emma never did anything by half measures, and she flung herself into restoring the little Admiral's health and self-confidence. For the first time since the loss of his arm, he stopped taking opium to make him sleep at nights, while the fresh air, the sunshine and Mrs Cadogan's Irish stews and English cooking brought him slowly back to health. In a series of chatty letters Emma dutifully reported back to Lady Nelson on her husband's health and progress, together with graphic details of the honours Naples and the Mediterranean states were bestowing on him.

The Grand Seigneur of Turkey created him the first member of a special Order of Knighthood he had founded for non-Mohammedans, sending him the badge of that Order, an enormous diamond surmounted by a plume of feathers taken from his own turban. Other presents included a white sable pelisse, and numerous gifts of money both for himself and the members of his fleet.

In England the City of London voted him a sword, the East India Company £2,000, Parliament a pension of £2,000 a year for life; and King George III created him Baron Nelson of the Nile, an honour which disappointed him as both Jervis and Howe had received viscountcies for victories which could not compare with his. He stifled his disappointment, but must have complained to Emma, for she scribbled a note to him: 'If I was the King of England I would make you the most noble puissant Duke Nelson, Marquis Nile, Earl Alexandria, Viscount Pyramid, Baron Crocodile and Prince Victory so that posterity might have you in all forms.'

It was a heady time and the future augured well. Ferdinand's army was in training, Sir William was busy supervising the packing of his crates of pictures and vases for loading aboard Nelson's storeships for the passage home, and the Austrian General Mack arrived, complete with a retinue of sixty, and five coachloads of personal luggage, to conduct the campaign. Nelson summed the general atmosphere up neatly when he wrote to Earl St Vincent, 'I am writing opposite Lady Hamilton, therefore you will not be surprised at the glorious jumble of this letter, was your Lordship in my place I much doubt that if you could write so well, our hearts and hands must be all in a flutter. Naples is a dangerous place and we must keep clear of it.' The letter may not have pleased St Vincent very much. He liked and respected Emma, and knew she had been of considerable help to the fleet. When he wrote to her, he addressed her as 'Dear Patroness of the Navy'. He also knew his Nelson, whom he regarded as a 'randy little man'. Thus he wrote to Emma: 'Pray do not let your fascinating Neapolitan dames approach too near him,' he instructed, 'for he is made of flesh and blood and cannot resist their temptations.' Nelson received a similar note, for St Vincent knew all about a certain mistress in Leghorn and believed, possibly with some justification, that one cause of the little Admiral's frequent lapses of health was more connected with that lady than with the rigours of naval life. 'I thank God that your health is restored and that the luscious Neapolitan dames have not impaired it.'

Sir William viewed the course of events with equanimity. The French had been beaten; Napoleon was marooned in Africa with his army and cut off from his supplies; his collections were mostly packed, and he hoped that by Christmas he and Emma would be home on leave in England, able to retire to his estates after spending a few days in London with his cronies at the Royal Society. He revelled in Nelson's presence as much as or even more than Emma. He thoroughly approved of him as a man and was grateful to him for restoring to him his position as the minister of a powerful country and a confidant of the Royal Family; there is no doubt that he regarded him as a favourite son as much as a personal friend. Nor did he see anything wrong in the fact that Emma and Nelson were so much together. She had never in their fourteen years together given him the slightest cause to worry, and at almost sixty-nine he had very little interest in sex anyway. He had aged considerably, and his health was still bad. 'He has turned into a very antique,' his friend the Earl Bishop had announced, and anyhow his chief delight in sensuality seems always to have been as an observer. No doubt he took pleasure from watching his thirty-eight-year-old wife become the object of Nelson's adulation.

While Sir William remained complacent, however, tongues were now beginning to wag with a vengeance. On 21 November the Queen invited a party of diplomats, together with leading members of the Court, to review

Ferdinand's army with whom he was now quartered. The camp was at San Germano and the Queen drove along the lines in a chariot and four, the carriages of her retinue following her. The Hamiltons and Nelson were in the Queen's chariot, and the Neapolitan historian Pietro Colletta remarked that it was not so much a parade of the troops as of Lady Hamilton parading her conquest over Nelson, who 'seated beside her in the same carriage appeared fascinated and submissive to her charms'. Despite the fact that at this stage the relationship was still completely innocent, the rumours grew more and more salacious and they soon reached Fanny Nelson in England. She in turn was not made to feel any happier about what was going on when her husband's letters started to arrive. Nelson was essentially a simple, open person and he wrote home in all innocence that Emma and Sir William were 'with the exception of you and my dear father the dearest friends I have in this world. I live as Sir William's son in the house and my glory is as dear to them as their own. In short I am under such obligations that I can never repay but with my eternal gratitude.'

In spite of himself Nelson was acutely conscious of his glory, and he began to welcome, even court, admiration, excusing himself any further self-analysis of his vanity by passing on his own adulation to Emma and the Queen. The Queen in turn, anxious to get her husband away at the head of his troops to drive the French out of Rome, grew more and more dependent on Nelson for his advice. For Ferdinand seemed quite happy to play at soldiers but not at all keen to go to war. As an excuse for not beginning hostilities he had refused to leave until his daughter the Princess Royal had had the baby which she was expecting: and when the infant arrived on 14 November, he further demurred, this time however on rather more substantial grounds.

Word had been received from the Austrians, who had already despatched General Mack: they were not now prepared to put troops into the field in support of Ferdinand unless it could clearly be shown that France was the aggressor. This was pertinent diplomacy, for despite the mobilisation and sabre-rattling of the Neapolitans, Naples and France were still parties to the truce which had so humiliated Ferdinand earlier in the year. The Austrian Queen, who was Ferdinand's daughter, was far more worried by Napoleon than she was by her simple-minded and idle father. At this juncture it would have been better for all concerned if the plan had been quietly dropped, but Nelson, relishing his newly adopted role of adviser to the Court, pressed the Court to continue. This was a posture which was totally out of character with all his previous behaviour, and can only be accounted for by the influence that the Queen and the Hamiltons had had upon him. Another contributory factor was that neither Nelson nor his hosts could return to England until the danger from the French in Rome had been removed. In all fairness, however, considerable influence was being brought to bear upon them to encourage Ferdinand in this rather foolish military adventure; a succession of letters from Lord Greville, the British Foreign Minister, told Nelson and Hamilton to push Ferdinand to the limit.

To force matters, Nelson went to the reluctant Royal warrior and publicly insulted him in front of his Court. He told the King that either he should advance with his sword in his hand and his trust in God, or he should shut up and resign himself to being thrown out of his Kingdom. Ferdinand swallowed the insult, and to salvage his pride led his army to Rome, while Nelson ferried a further five thousand Neapolitan troops to Leghorn so that they could attack the French in the rear. The result was a complete fiasco from start to finish. As far as Nelson could judge, no one had bothered to tell the Governor of Leghorn he was coming, or that a war with the French was imminent. (In a farewell note, Emma had shown him that she was aware of the attractions Leghorn held for him, and had heavily underlined her instruction, 'Do not go ashore at Leghorn, there is no comfort there for you.') What had also been ignored was that Leghorn was both a part of the separate state of Tuscany, and neutral. Nelson eventually landed his troops and sailed back to Naples in disgust at the inefficiency of all concerned.

Ferdinand's campaign was even more lunatic. General Mack was a gentleman, and regretted the rather ungentlemanly decision to attack the French without first declaring war, so he remedied the discourtesy by writing to the French General, Championnet, in Rome. He also sent the French his plans; this meant that the French could pull their troops out of harm's way, as they were well aware of Austria's attitude and had no wish to give the Neapolitans the slightest excuse for calling the French the 'aggressors'. Leaving a token garrison of five hundred men in Rome, the French withdrew thirty miles to the north of the city.

Ferdinand entered Rome in triumph and for ten days pillaged the treasures of the Vatican, while his men went on a wild spree of rape, murder and looting. Then collecting up his army he began to look for the elusive French. At the first encounter, the Neapolitans began to desert in thousands. By mid-December Ferdinand realised that his cause was lost and he hurriedly left the city, accompanied only by some close friends. He changed clothes with one of his courtiers, the Duke of Ascoli, and rushed back to Naples in disguise, abandoning his army to the French. With neither supplies nor officers, his troops began to ravage the countryside. General Mack, who was engaged in packing his carriages with luggage, was surrounded by the French and gave up without a fight.

The arrival of the King, wearing only the clothes he stood up in—and those borrowed—alarmed Naples. The Royal Family evacuated themselves to Caserta and wondered what was to become of them while the *lazzaroni* clamoured outside the walls of the Palace, shouting for arms with which to defend themselves against the French. The Queen—now with a new-born grandchild—appealed to Emma, Sir William and Nelson for advice and assistance. The Hamiltons began packing their few remaining possessions. Nelson, pondering what course of action to take, had his mind made up for him. A messenger to him from the Queen, a Signor Ferrari, had been seized by the mob in the belief that he was a French spy. He had been beaten and stabbed to death, but the incident was reported to Nelson as an indication of the mob's determination to rise against the Royal Family. It seemed that the *lazzaroni* were about to behave in the same way as their Parisian counterparts. He had two choices: either he could land his sailors and marines, fortify the city and defy the French; or he could retreat. He chose the latter. He signalled the dispersed elements of his squadron to join him at once, as 'things are in such a critical state', and made his detailed plans to evacuate the Royal Family and the Hamiltons to Palermo in Sicily. It was a most un-Nelsonian decision, as was his secret signal to Captain Troubridge who was lying outside Leghorn: 'Everything is as bad as possible. For God's sake make haste.'

VII

December 1798–June 1799

Mutual Dishonour

'We weep together
this is our only comfort.'
*Emma, Lady Hamilton
to Charles Greville*

Nelson had misjudged the situation, as indeed Maria Carolina had intended he should. He failed to realise that the *lazzaroni* were not hostile to the Royal Family, but to the French and the pro-French elements among the middle classes. The demonstrations outside the Palace were—for all their sickening violence—demonstrations of loyalty, and a plea for the family to stay with them and hold off the French. Sir William could have clarified the situation, but he was preoccupied with the loading of his collections. Nelson was subsequently to realise that he had been manoeuvred into his decision to evacuate the Royal Family to Sicily, and he covered both himself and Sir William in his report to St Vincent by stating that it would have been 'highly imprudent' for either of them to have been seen anywhere near the Palace, as there were strong rumours that the Jacobins intended to seize them both as hostages against any British naval bombardment should the French take Naples.

Although it might have been imprudent to go ashore or to visit the Queen, Nelson had not been so negligent as to omit to make a contingency plan for evacuation. In fact two months before, on 3 October, he had foreseen that just such a situation might arise, and together with Acton and the Queen, with either Sir William or Emma translating, had prepared a detailed plan. All that remained was to put it into effect. Before this could be done, however, Ferdinand threw a Royal spanner into the preparations: he categorically refused to leave unless the entire Treasury was taken with him. Nelson, already encumbered by three transports full of Sir William's and his friends' possessions, and two more full of French Royalist refugees, wearily agreed. The problem was how to clear the Royal Treasury without the citizens of Naples finding out. The Queen and Emma provided the solution.

Naples had grown accustomed to the sight of wagons carrying Sir William's possessions from the Palazzo Sessa to the harbour. The wagons had been borrowed from the Royal stables, so they were obliged to make a triangular journey: from the stables to the Palazzo, the Palazzo to the harbour, and thence back to the stables before returning empty to the Palazzo again. Now on the third, empty, leg of the journey, they were loaded with treasure. This was delivered loose to Emma, who supervised the packing. Gold coin, silver, jewels, fine bronzes, bales of velvet; the list was enormous. The wagons kept up their monotonous round for eight days and nights, and Emma packed everything into casks and bales, marking it as naval stores or as Sir William's property. Not content with robbing his own Treasury, Ferdinand insisted on carrying with him all the coin and plate that the Neapolitans had voluntarily contributed for the defence of the city. Nelson duly reported to St Vincent:

'... from 14 December ... the danger for the personal safety of their Sicilian Majesties was daily increasing; and new treasons were found out, even to the Minister of War. The whole correspondence relative to this important business was carried on with the greatest address by Lady Hamilton and the Queen, who having been in constant habits of correspondence, no one could suspect them. Lady Hamilton from that time to the 21st every night received the jewels of the Royal Family etc. etc. and such clothes as might be necessary for the very large party about to embark, to the amount I am confident, of full two millions five hundred thousand pounds sterling.'

The treasure was stored in the hold of Nelson's flagship, the *Vanguard*, and described on the loading bills as salt pork and biscuits. The arrangements for the evacuation of the Royal Family were just as secret and even more complicated, the plan being jointly drawn up by Nelson and Prince Francesco Caracciolo, the Admiral of the Neapolitan fleet. The latter did not see eye to eye with Nelson as the two men were jealous of each other; Caracciolo was annoyed that the treasure was to go on a British ship, and he was further snubbed when the King insisted on travelling with Nelson instead of on his own flagship. Nevertheless Caracciolo prepared an excellent plan and it worked well.

A secret passage led from the Palace to the quayside, and the first task was for Emma and the Neapolitan Admiral to explore it to see if it was still serviceable. It was dark, damp and eerie, but perfectly usable for the escape. It was arranged that the Royal party would split into two and come down the passage at two-hourly intervals. Caracciolo's written embarkation order was extremely detailed; it survives to this day, in the translation Emma made for Nelson:

'First Embarkation
The King
The Queen
Prince Leopold
Prince Alberto, and nurse
Three Princesses
General Acton
Prince Castelcicala [sic]
Prince Belmonte
Count Thurn
The Hereditary Prince
His Princess
Their daughter and nurse
Duke of Gravina

This embarkation should be made at the Molesiglio at eight o'clock and a half in the night.

Second Embarkation
Dr Ulderica Sanchez
D. Ma. Giuseppa Bartoldy } Her Majesteyes
Madame Chatelain
Da Rosa, e.d. Guiseppa Pucci—the Princesses
Mlle. Baselli,
The first nurse to the child   The Princess Hereditarye's
D. Gius Garano   King's Confessor
D. Michele Troja—Surgeon
D. Vin. Falco   }
D. Niccola de Pietro } King's Attendants
D. Gius Vitta }
Abbe Labdan }   Prince's do
Losinese }   for the young Princes
Eccevina }
M. Pernt   Cook
Gaet. Lombardo and Son   Cook
Leop. Caprioli and Son   Ripostieri
John Kenish   }
Savari Salvante }   Servants'

Nelson's own orders were just as detailed:

'Most Secret
    Three barges, and the small cutter of the *Alcmene*, armed with cutlasses only, to be at the *Victoria* at half past seven o'clock precisely. Only one barge to be at the wharf, the others to lay on their oars at the outside of the rocks—the small barge of the *Vanguard* to be at the wharf. The above boats to be on board the *Alcmene* before seven o'clock, under the direction of Captain Hope. Grapnels to be in the boats.
    All other boats of the *Vanguard* and *Alcmene* to be armed with cutlasses, and the launches with carronades to assemble on board the *Vanguard*, under direction of Captain Hardy, and to put off from her at half-past eight o'clock precisely, to row half-way towards the Mola

Figlio. These boats to have four or six soldiers in them. In case assistance is wanted by me, false fires will be burnt.

Nelson

The *Alcmene* to be ready to slip in the night, if necessary.'

Meanwhile General Acton arranged that one of the King's equerries, Count Thurn, should meet Nelson's party at the quayside entrance of the tunnel, and if all was ready should give him the password 'All goes right and well.' If there had been a snag, Nelson would be told 'All is wrong, you may go back.' By now many Neapolitans suspected that the Royal Family were about to desert them, but they reasoned that Nelson would not sail without the Hamiltons. Here again Sir William, Emma and her mother provided a useful diversion. On the evening of 21 December they left their Palazzo, which was brightly lit, entered their carriage and drove with a full retinue of servants to a diplomatic reception being given by the Turkish Ambassador. When they arrived, they told the coachmen and outriders to come back in two hours to take them home, and ordered the servants to prepare a small supper to be waiting for them on their return. The orders were heard by the crowd of onlookers watching the arrival of the guests and no suspicions were aroused. What no one knew was that the brightly lit Palazzo was almost empty, and that no sooner had Sir William and his party had a welcoming drink, than they mystified the astonished Ambassador by donning their cloaks and slipping out of the back door, to walk briskly down to the harbour where they were rowed out to the *Vanguard*.

While the crowds were watching the reception at the Turkish Embassy, Nelson's party was rowing silently up to the quay. Nelson, cloaked, sword in hand, rendezvoused with Count Thurn, and on learning that all was well climbed up the dim stairway and into the Royal apartments where the Royal Family, ranging from the King to his baby grandson who was still at his nurse's breast, were waiting for him. By midnight everyone was safely aboard the *Vanguard*.

The *Vanguard* was quite literally packed from stem to stern. There were boxes of treasure everywhere, and the Royal party milled around in a state of total confusion. The King insisted on occupying the wardroom all to himself and Mrs Cadogan made his bed up for him. Apart from that the King took relatively little interest in what was going on, and spent his time discussing the prospects of arranging some hunting in Sicily with his personal gamekeeper whom he had insisted on bringing along. The Queen, her children and the other ladies in the entourage occupied Nelson's cabin, the Queen sitting in the only chair moaning to herself, her eldest daughter weeping in Nelson's cot, while the children and the others sat on the floor. Emma made them all beds, and her mother prepared some stew and broth. That first night was uncomfortable, but compared with what was to follow it was a picnic.

When dawn broke over Naples, the populace found that the Palace was empty and that Nelson's fleet was anchored far out in the bay, well out of range of the cannon which protected the city on the seaward side. Nevertheless hundreds of boats rowed out to the *Vanguard*, some full of people clamouring for a place on board, others crying on the King to return and save them from the French. The King turned a deaf ear to their cries. 'Tell them,' he said, 'that I will return when the populace have done their duty.' Although he refused to return, he could not depart, as a strong on-shore wind had sprung up. The fleet rolled heavily at anchor, waiting for the wind to change direction. The overladen *Vanguard* rolled so heavily that most of the passengers were sick and the King's confessor fell and broke his arm. The wind held steady for forty-eight hours, and it was not until the evening of 23 December that it changed direction, and the ill-assorted convoy made unsteady sail for Sicily.

By now, many of the men on board the Neapolitan ships commanded by Prince Caracciolo had deserted, and at least ten of these had not men enough to take them to sea. Nelson ordered them to be manned by skeleton crews, and if or when the French arrived they were to be burnt. It was

the final insult to his rival for the Royal affections;
Caracciolo, with some justification, began to sulk and
wonder where his loyalties really lay.

The voyage to Palermo was to prove the most difficult
sea passage of Nelson's career. On Christmas Eve a
tremendous storm blew up, and it was all the *Vanguard*
could do to keep afloat. The wind blew out her topsails and
brought down her foretopmast, while the sea crashed over
the sides and flowed freely down below the decks. Sailors
stood lashed to bulkwarks, armed with axes ready to cut
away the mass of sail and cordage which kept crashing
down. The disorder below was appalling. The Royal
Family lay on the floor of the great cabin in wretched and
retching misery. Sir William retired to the surgeon's cabin
and sat there with a loaded pistol in each hand, explaining
that he was prepared to blow his brains out rather than
drown. He could not bear the thought of the undignified
death which he believed the 'gurgle gurgle' of the sea had
in store for him. While Sir William worried about his
dignity the Count D'Esterhazy, the Imperial Ambassador
from Vienna, struggled manfully on to the deck. He was
worried by his conscience. He had a gold snuff-box with a
miniature of his mistress painted in the nude set into its lid;
in order to make his peace with God, he flung it into the
sea.

Throughout the storm, which lasted all night and right
through Christmas Day, Emma alone looked after the
Royal Family. She fed them, she nursed them, she mopped
their brows with rags soaked in vinegar; she cuddled and
comforted the children. It was perhaps her finest hour, but
more tragedy was in store. Towards evening, the Queen's
youngest son, the six-year-old Prince Alberto who had
been the most affected by sea sickness, went into a series of
convulsions, and just as the storm abated and the
mountains of Sicily appeared on the horizon, he died
moaning in Emma's arms. The Queen, prostrate with
grief, lay on the floor in the vomit, vinegar, spilt food and
the seawater which had cascaded through the hatches,
throwing herself into a fit of hysterics, when a somewhat

tactless note arrived from Nelson.

'My dear Lady Hamilton,

I shall most certainly expect the happiness of seeing you, Sir William and Mrs Cadogan at dinner. Come, let us have as merry an Xmas as circumstances will admit, and believe me ever, yours most truly, Nelson.'

Whether or not the Hamiltons accepted the invitation is not recorded, but what we do know is that when the *Vanguard* dropped her anchor off Palermo at 2 am on Boxing Day 1798, only Nelson and Emma stood on the quarterdeck. Both were exhausted, but both had an overwhelming sense of having done their duty. Each basked in the other's admiration; Emma for Nelson's seamanship, Nelson for Emma's courage and devotion to their Royal charges. Ahead of them, in a bleak December dawn, was the city of Palermo. It had as fine a situation as Naples but it was essentially a summer city. In December, though it boasted an almost African climate, it was plagued by cold winds and excessive humidity. As the *Vanguard* came to a standstill, the sea was calm, the storm was over, and in that silence perhaps both Emma and Nelson realised that their future was to be a shared one.

Nelson and Sir William both knew that they were in disgrace at home. Their counsel to launch Ferdinand against the French had been disastrous and both felt their honour was at stake. Emma was probably happier; she felt important, or perhaps—and for the first time in her life—needed. She was no longer a tool, a plaything, an exhibit. She was, and had doubly proved herself to be, an essential part of and a tower of strength to the two men who meant most to her, as well as to the Queen who by her sly generosity had given her the status and position that society at home in England had withheld.

The Queen went ashore immediately, carrying her children and her grief with her. Ferdinand insisted on remaining aboard until an appropriate Royal reception was arranged. He was rowed ashore with full pomp and ceremony the following morning, receiving a King's welcome with what Nelson described as 'the loudest exclamations and *apparent* joy' from his Sicilian subjects. His first act was to issue a proclamation that anyone poaching the Royal game preserves would be sentenced to the galleys.

Sir William, Emma and Nelson were quartered in the Villa Bastioni. It was cold, there were no fires, and there was precious little furniture; Sir William promptly went down with yet another chill and bilious fever, Nelson busied himself with his paperwork, and Emma went to comfort the Queen. In their spare moments, they all appear to have been writing letters, and they all in their own ways give us a vivid picture of their respective situations.

The most important letter to survive is that which Maria Carolina wrote to her daughter in Vienna, although for diplomatic reasons it was posted to the Neapolitan Ambassador there. She wrote in cypher, using lemon juice as her ink:

'The most unhappy of Queens, mothers and women, writes this to you. I say the most unhappy because I feel everything so acutely and I doubt if I shall survive what has happened to me during the last forty days. We fled from Naples on Friday. The arrangements for burning the ships kept us till Sunday in the harbour, where we received deputations that came to harangue us to try and make us return, but never thought of arming themselves to defend us. Mack came on board Sunday morning, half-dead, weeping, exclaiming that all was lost, that treason and cowardice were at their height and that his only consolation was to see us on board Nelson's ship. The sailors fled from the ship; at last we had to put English and Portuguese sailors to replace them. At least 1,500 sailors fled in one night. The Portuguese remained behind in the harbour to burn, to my eternal grief, our beautiful Navy, which has cost us so much. We set sail at eight hours of the evening. Our misfortunes are such that I wish to die! To begin with the most essential, at Palermo people seemed pleased to see us but not enthusiastic. The nobles crowded round; they seem to have no desire but to obtain all they can and my heart tells me that if the Emperor does not soon put himself in action it will not be four months before we are forced out of Sicily as we were out of Naples. I would offer these vultures all the jewels and treasures which we have with us, if they would only leave us to live and die in peace . . . Indeed, I feel desperate. I vow to you I do not think I can live in this condition. I do not believe I shall survive. In the name of God, arrange for my unhappy daughters to go to Vienna where marriages can be arranged for them or they can retire to the Convent of the Visitation. My daughter-in-law is very ill with her chest; she is not likely to survive. Their father, though I should not speak of that, does not seem to feel anything except what concerns himself personally and not much of that, or to realise that he has lost the best part of his crown and his revenues. He only takes notice of the novelties that amuse him, without thinking that we are reduced to a quarter of our revenue, dishonoured, unhappy, and have led others into the same unhappiness . . . Indeed, I am in despair, I do not think I shall survive. Everything displeases me here, all I love best has gone. The civilities here are such as would be given to a King who has lost everything. I think no more of grandeur, nor of glory, nor of honours, I only think to live retired in a corner.

The details of all our suffering will make you tremble. It has really been beyond my strength to endure, and I feel that I shall not survive. Friday 21st following a revolt in the town, people killed and wounded under the windows of the King, talk of the people confiscating the castles, the arms, and forbidding anyone to leave the city, flight was decided upon. What I suffered during the rest of this day cannot be expressed. There was a cold north wind as we left at night. I trembled like a leaf. Without my virtuous and attached Mimi I should have fallen a thousand times. Think of the horror of this, with six children and my young daughter-in-law and an infant at the breast! We arrived on board all rigid with cold and I half-insensible with unhappiness. We passed that first night without bed, without light, fire or supper. Saturday, the 22nd, began with a letter from the deputation, everyone demanding to speak to the King, who would see no one. The wretched day passed in this misery and my heart was torn. We tried everywhere to find what was necessary for so many children accustomed to every luxury, but in vain... We raised anchor at eight o'clock in the evening. At midnight the bad weather commenced, but the storm did not really break till Monday, the 24th. We were all the voyage lying on the ground, eleven of us in the demi-poop, the women half-unconscious, Lady Hamilton kept bringing us vinegar and basins in which to vomit. At one o'clock after midday there came such a tempest that the sails were all torn to shreds, both in our vessel and that of Caracciolo. We began to think ourselves lost. The mast broke, the sailors were climbing about with hatchets to cut down the damaged rigging.

Louise was in her chemise on her knees, Amelia demanding a confessor who would come to give her absolution, Leopold the same. I felt so unhappy to think of what had happened and what must happen yet, that I saw death come without regret, trusting in the Divine Mercy and content to perish with my children. Towards two o'clock the danger ceased and Nelson said that in the thirty years he had been at sea he had never seen such a storm, a wind and tempest. When night came the sea was so heavy that everything had to be roped. We remained still on the ground. Tuesday, Christmas Day, the storm diminished a little, and at nine o'clock little Alberto, aged six years and a half, who had never suffered from convulsions, though so very delicate, suddenly took one so strong that, though he had never vomited, he died at half past seven in the evening in the midst of us, despite all our remedies. Let any mother judge of my feelings. His dear little corpse stayed with us until five o'clock in the morning, when we arrived, and I hastened to disembark. The town of Palermo is large, the Palace uninhabited, inconvenient, cold, lacking everything, neither chairs, nor bed, nor sofa, nor anything. One half-furnished apartment, which was warmed, had to serve for my daughter-in-law and her child. The former is very sickly, but I hope to prolong her life. I have been bled, all my children are ill, nobody has yet recovered from the voyage. I have besides, the frightful loss of my child and that of our realm. The King is well, the Prince the same. The Princess suffers with her chest and keeps coughing. My daughters and Leopold are sad, overcome, suffering, and think as I do. I have seen little here, but everything affects me, and I believe I cannot live long here; I am convinced that I shall succumb, and my death is indifferent to me, if I can see my six daughters and Leopold established in some religious institution in Austria. I see everything black. Give all these frightful and truthful details to the Empress, my daughter.

I feel everything, as I alone can feel. I foresaw all and no one would listen to me. Religion can alone support me. Italy is in the hands of barbarians, our commerce is ruined. Further, for the climax of unhappiness, the few effects and the goods we saved have been lost in the tempest. I do not even like to think how many honest people have perished—only the diamonds are saved. I should have preferred to have kept more useful furnishings. As for me, I am in true despair, convinced that Sicily will soon follow the example of Naples, and that we shall lose life and honour. If the sea voyage were not so long I would try to get to Austria, but I fear too much to lose another child. The King passes my comprehension. He has already taken a little house in the country. Prince Jaci is his factotum. He goes each evening to the theatre or the masked ball and is gay and content, is irritated if anyone talks to him of Naples, will not give any audiences, will not show himself officially in any public place, he grumbles at anyone who mentions business to him and speaks as if nothing had happened; therefore they all despise him and do as they please. I am quite sure I shall perish here; I cannot live much longer and my children will remain without a mother, abandoned orphans. O blessed tempest, why do you not engulf us all?'

In his turn, Sir William wrote to Grevillle, bitterly blaming the French, the Austrians and everyone else for his misfortunes, and suggesting that it was time he retired. 'I feel age creeping upon me, but I will bear up as long and as well as I can, and not giving up as my father did twenty years before he died, calling himself a dying man—and so we all are.' Emma wrote to Greville as well, lamenting the loss of all she had had to leave behind and the sorry condition of the Queen at Naples. 'We weep together,' she wrote, 'this is our only comfort.' She also remarked that Sir William and the King were both philosophers, a cryptic reference to the fact that each was now solely concerned with his own comfort. 'Nothing affects them thank God, and we are scolded—even for showing proper sensibility.'

Emma and the Queen were now closer than ever before. It was not only a case of one woman comforting another in their mutual grief; there were even sterner realities to face. Ferdinand, having frittered away his Kingdom, now—and with some justification it must be admitted—blamed his Queen for all that had happened. He was determined to govern on his own and he isolated her from his counsels. He now also regarded Emma as a nuisance and an enemy and frequently lost his temper with her, on one occasion even threatening to throw her out of a window. However, although he arrogated all powers to himself he did nothing with them, and continued to spend his time hunting and throwing parties. As he had the entire Neapolitan treasury at his disposal (the Queen had greatly exaggerated the extent of the losses at sea), the standard and the cost of living in Palermo rocketed. The Sicilians, infinitely more sophisticated and cynical than the Neapolitans, cheerfully joined in all his festivities and devoted themselves to relieving him of as much of his loot as they could. Ferdinand cared little for Naples and even less for his wife and family.

The Queen rightly saw that at the rate Ferdinand was spending money, the hospitality of the Sicilian nobility would evaporate in four or five months at the most: in fact as soon as the King was broke. Already they were sniggering behind his back, while the peasants had little love for either their Spanish-born King or his Austrian wife. In Sicily there were no *lazzaroni* to buoy up Ferdinand's popularity, or to keep the nobility in check. The limbo which so obviously awaited the Neapolitan Court was a terrifying one, and Maria Carolina was determined somehow to recover her husband's kingdom. Again she used Emma as her tool and this time, through Emma, she had Nelson and the British fleet as well.

The news from Naples could not have been worse. On 8 January the French arrived at the gates of the city, and in compliance with Nelson's previous instructions the Neapolitan fleet was burnt. The Neapolitan nobility who had stayed made an ignominious armistice with the French and allowed them into the city but the *lazzaroni* refused to accept the terms of the armistice and hand-to-hand fighting raged in the streets. General Championnet who commanded the French forces eventually overcame their resistance, but at considerable loss, and some five thousand *lazzaroni* were killed. The remainder then gave themselves over to looting, even sacking the Royal Palace, though out of deference to their absent monarch they agreed to do so for only three hours.

Once General Championnet had crushed the *lazzaroni*, he established a Republic which with a neat sense of the antique he christened the Parthenopean Republic, and many of the city's intelligentsia flocked to serve it. The new Republic's first governors, appointed on 22 January 1799, were a well-meaning but hopelessly inexperienced band of idealists. France promised them support but the French ideas of Republicanism and those of the Neapolitans differed wildly. French commissioners arrived and began sequestrating almost every asset they could find. What money was left in the country was seized, works of art, even statues from the public squares, were hauled off to Paris, and anyone suspected of Royalist sympathies was thrown into jail. Within a month the new administration was in dire trouble with the populace, and the French military presence could do very little about it.

The occupying army had lost a third of its strength from venereal disease, and over four hundred French soldiers had already been stabbed in the back in the dark alleyways of the city.

On learning of what was going on, Maria Carolina made a determined bid to regain her power. Fortunately for her, Ferdinand had quickly lost interest in anything to do with government, and his natural laziness made her task easy. Her first action was to bring Nelson firmly on to the centre of the stage, and for the next few months he was more of a Prime Minister to the Bourbon Court than a British Admiral. Whether out of love for Emma or the Queen, or more probably from a deep-rooted sense of obligation for the ruin which Sir William's and his own counsels had brought upon them, he saw himself as absolutely committed to returning the Royal Family to their throne. He was to write to Fanny in England that, 'Good Sir William, Lady Hamilton and myself are the mainsprings of the machine which manage what is going on in this country. We are all bound for England when we can quit our posts with propriety.'

Emma's first task was to send out inflammatory leaflets, which had been written by the Queen, to be distributed in Naples. These, which urged the populace to rise against the French, were slipped into Sir William's diplomatic bag and sent to the British consuls in Capua and Leghorn for onward transmission to Naples. Another task was to act as interpreter for Nelson in the Council Chamber, and to act as hostess and charmer to the many nobles from whom the Queen wished to solicit support. Sir William moved from his draughty villa to a fifty-roomed palace which more than befitted his station. He and Nelson shared the expenses; at some time in mid-February they began to share Emma as well.

The palace soon became a giddy, heady and in some ways a disgraceful establishment. The feverish excitement and constant intrigue went to everyone's head. The Sicilians loved gambling, and almost every night after dinner, Sir William's palace was full of erstwhile supporters of the Queen's cause busily playing for high stakes. Emma grew strident and vain, and all the polish which both Greville and Sir William had instilled in her slipped away in the intoxicating atmosphere of the Sicilian spring. Nelson himself was the most swollen-headed of the three, appearing every day in every conceivable decoration that he could manage to pin on to his uniform, and constantly reminding everyone he met of his fame, his triumphs and his importance. Lord Montgomery, who was passing through Palermo, was entertained by the Hamiltons and has left a penetrating account of his first introduction to Nelson:

'The hero of the Nile now came forth from a corner where he had been writing ... after a few trifling queries ... Lord Nelson said to me—"Pray, Sir, have you heard about the battle of the Nile?... *That* battle sir was the most extraordinary one that was ever fought, and it is *unique*, Sir, for three reasons; first for its having been fought at night; secondly for its having been fought at anchor; and thirdly for its having been gained by an Admiral with one arm." To each of these reasons I made a profound bow; but had the speech been made after dinner, I should have imagined the hero had imbibed an extra dose of champagne.'

Sir William came in for his share of Montgomery's strictures, being described as 'a perfect Neapolitan in mind and manners. The consequence he retained as an Ambassador was derived from his wife's intrigues; but as long as he could keep his situation, draw his salary and collect vases, he cared little about politics; he left the management of that to her ladyship.' These are cruel cameos, but probably accurate enough. Both Nelson and Emma were living at the last stretch of their nerves. The British Embassy was the hub of all that had to be done, and there was much to do. The card parties and masked balls for which historians have blamed Emma cannot have lasted long. There was a fleet to administer and maintain, and a future to be planned. By early spring, at Nelson and

Emma's instigation, the Court had mounted a counter-revolution.

This time the squabbling generals and admirals were ignored. Prince Caracciolo had made matters easy by asking permission to return to Naples in order to prevent his property from being sequestered by the French. On his arival he had promptly joined the Republicans and rapidly rose in rank to command their navy. With the Prince turned traitor, the Court had a free choice as to who should lead the Royalist counter-attack. Curiously, it fell on a senior member of the Church, Cardinal Fabrizio Ruffo. Nelson thought him a conceited little man, but the Cardinal knew his Neapolitans, and with the pragmatism of his race and cloth suggested launching a holy war against the French. Nelson's ships slipped him ashore well to the south of Naples and within days he was at the head of a rabble of peasants who called themselves the 'Army of the Holy Faith'. Ruffo did not enlighten his men that his rank of cardinal was a political sinecure and that he had no formal clerical qualifications. It mattered little, for his rabble was probably the most blood-thirsty crew ever let loose into southern Italy. Nelson dubbed him the 'Great Devil who has charge of the Christian Army'; still, Ruffo swept all before him and by the end of May he was besieging Naples from the south. In support of this operation, Nelson sent one of his toughest and most unscrupulous commanders, Captain Troubridge, to blockade Naples itself. Troubridge, a tradesman's son who had worked his way up in the Navy by a combination of ruthlessness and sheer cold courage, took his duties seriously. Appropriately his ship was the *Culloden*, and his mission was to stamp out the Jacobins on the islands in the Bay of Naples.

Troubridge wrought bloody vengeance upon all he captured on Ischia and Capri. Most of his prisoners went to immediate execution, but Troubridge scorned even to let them die on proper gallows, as providing such an amenity 'would be menial work for the fleet'. Troubridge's gleeful reports to Nelson of the 'heads he had taken' are a stain on both Nelson and the Royal Navy.

Nelson himself made two fruitless sorties from Palermo in chase of an elusive French fleet, and maintained a rigid blockade of Malta. No one could accuse him of neglecting his duties, even though he interpreted these duties as having rather more to do with serving Maria Carolina than the Lords of the Admiralty. The French themselves were busy drawing in their horns. In early April, a joint Austro-Russian army marched into Italy, driving the French before them. The occcupation force in Naples was withdrawn except for a token garrison, and by midsummer Cardinal Ruffo's army had stormed its way into the heart of Naples itself. Nelson was not there to support him, but he was represented by one English frigate, the *Seahorse*, commanded by Captain Edward Foote. Two thousand Republican sympathisers took refuge in the twin castles which dominate Naples, the Castel dell'Uovo and Castel Nuovo, while the token French garrison locked itself up in the military barracks of Fort St Elmo, whose guns guarded the Bay of Naples itself. Each hoped that a French fleet would come to their rescue, for the only sign of the British was Foote in his little frigate, hovering safely out of cannon shot, and Troubridge who was busy massacring the priests on Capri whom he believed to be Republican at heart. Troubridge also complained to Nelson that he needed another judge to expedite the trials and executions. The judge he had was evidently either too slow or had some scruples about his task for Troubridge wrote, 'The judge appears to me to be the poorest creature I ever saw, frightened out of his senses, says seventy families are concerned and talks of it being necessary to have a bishop degrade them before he can execute them. I told him to hang them first and if he did not think the degradation of hanging sufficient, I would piss on the D.....d Jacobin's carcase.'

It was all over bar the reprisals. Ruffo agreed a capitulation with the besieged Republicans and the French, which Captain Foote signed on behalf of his absent commander. It was a gentlemanly and generous agreement, the magnanimous terms of which enabled Ferdinand to return sure of the support of the nobility who hitherto had hated and resented him. On hearing the news, Ferdinand refused to go to Naples but sent Nelson in his place as his personal representative. The Queen was forbidden by Ferdinand to return, so she in turn appointed Emma as her representative. On the evening of 23 June, almost six months to the day since their ignominious departure, Nelson and Emma were together aboard his flagship and anchored in sight of the city. Sir William was with them, but this time in no official capacity.

There were some differences. Nelson had a new flagship, the *Foudroyant*; he was also in an appalling temper. He was on the verge of salving his honour, at least to his own way of thinking, by returning Ferdinand to his throne; but his honour was also troubling him in another direction, for with him he now had Emma in an entirely different capacity. Before he had admired her, now he loved her. Before he had been her courtier, now she was his mistress. Much the most sobering thought was the news which Emma had for him as a consequence of their affair, and equally worrying was the question of how much Sir William realised of what was going on.

VIII

June 1799–November 1800

Revenge and Return

'Nelson, thy flag haul down
Hang up thy laurel crown
While her we sing.
No more in triumph swell
Since that with her you dwell
And don't her William tell
Nor George your King.'

Broadsheet published on
Nelson's return to England,
6 November 1800

The affair between Nelson and Emma had started almost
by accident on the evening of 12 February. Nelson had
been given a puppy by the captain of a Turkish ship who
had visited Palermo in order to pay his respects to the
King, and also to deliver a letter and a gold snuff-box
studded with diamonds which had been sent to the
Admiral by the Emperor of Russia. The captain's name
was Amir, and Nelson, who had a childish penchant for
anagrams, promptly christened the pup Mira. The
Hamiltons gave a dinner party for the Turk, and the drink
flowed much too freely. The Turk began to boast of his
exploits, and drawing his scimitar boasted how he had
decapitated twenty Frenchmen in a single day. Emma
promptly kissed the sword, and a Mrs Lock who was the

wife of the British Consul either fainted or pretended to do so. Emma refused to leave the table and attend to her, claiming that Mrs Lock was shamming.

The Locks disliked the Hamiltons, and were part of a clique who took pleasure in writing derogatory letters home about Sir William and his wife. Emma was probably quite correct in treating Mrs Lock's apparent swoon with disdain. However, some of the Locks' cronies cried 'shame' and even hissed. Sir William was deeply embarrassed, and after dinner Emma went to Nelson— probably after having had words with her husband over her behaviour. It is most unlikely that she intended to seduce him: she was upset and overwrought, and to console her Nelson let her cuddle the puppy. It seems that one thing led to another. The affair lasted for two months, to be terminated when Nelson left on one of his abortive chases after the French fleet. At this time Sir William was unaware of what had happened, and the relationship was not renewed when Nelson returned. In early June, believing herself to be two months pregnant, Emma confided in the Queen who sent her personal physician Dr Troya to give her a 'douche'. Then on the six-day voyage to Naples, Emma told Nelson what had happened, but claimed she had had a miscarriage. The little Admiral was both ridden with guilt and, childless as he was, bitterly sad at the loss of what might have been his child. He and Emma—partly in order to fool Sir William—referred to the baby which might have been as Mira. Two years later, Nelson was to write to Emma as he sailed to do battle with the Danes at Copenhagen: 'For these two nights I have done nothing but dream of you, the first I saw your tears as plain as possible on your left cheek ... last night I thought that poor Mira was alive and between us, what can this mean? Time will discover.'

In the great cabin of the *Foudroyant*, Nelson, Sir William and Emma took their evening meal together, afterwards going up the quarterdeck shortly before the dusk drew in. Sir William was tired and despondent. He had received news that one of Nelson's storeships, the *Colossus*, had been wrecked off the Scilly Isles, and that many of his most precious vases and pictures had been lost. In his way he had lost something as dear to him as any child. Now from his vantage point on the ship he could see his Palazzo, looted by the mob, and a gaping hole caused by a French shell where his study had been. He handed the telescope to Nelson, who was already in a black and ugly temper, his stump jigging up and down, a sure sign of an imminent explosion. After examining the ruin of the Palazzo Sessa he trained the glass on the twin forts in which the Republicans had taken refuge and was infuriated to see that they were still flying the Republican flag. When it was explained to him by the unfortunate Captain Foote that this was in accordance with the armistice which Cardinal Ruffo had agreed with the rebels, and which Foote had signed on his Admiral's behalf, Nelson exploded.

He immediately sent Captains Troubridge and Ball ashore to inform the Cardinal that the armistice was annulled, and ordered Captain Foote to haul down his own flag of truce. Ruffo refused to discuss Neapolitan affairs with two relatively junior naval officers, and the following morning rowed out to discuss the matter with Nelson. Sir William and Emma acted as interpreters. The Cardinal was far too suave a negotiator for the irascible Nelson. He pointed out that it was he who had taken Naples, not the Admiral, that the terms of the armistice were just and honourable and that they had been signed not only by Captain Foote, but had also been both approved and signed by emissaries from Britain's other allies, Austria, Russia and Turkey. Nelson refused to haggle with him, sending him ashore with the message that the Republicans must surrender unconditionally and were to come out of the castles 'to be hanged or otherwise disposed of as their sovereign thought proper'. Nelson's attitude created havoc in the city and the Republicans decided to stay where they were. Meanwhile the chief of the *lazzaroni* rowed out to the *Foudroyant*. Emma spotted him and told Nelson who he was, and he was promptly invited aboard. He claimed to have ninety thousand of his slum-living ruffians ready to take the castles, but the French had seized all their arms. The number impressed Nelson, who lent him a hundred marines and armed several hundred of his followers. They were instructed to spread the word that the armistice was annulled, and to tear down the terms of the agreement from all the walls of the city where Ruffo had posted them. At the same time Nelson sent Ball and Troubridge ashore with a note to Ruffo which stated: 'Lord Nelson begs me to assure Your Eminence that he is resolved to do nothing to break the armistice that Your Excellence has accorded the Castles of Naples.'

This ambiguous note convinced the Cardinal that all was well, and the Republicans were given two choices. They could opt for exile, in which case they could board the transports in the bay and sail to Toulon, or they could return to their own homes. Most chose exile, and oblivious to their danger, boarded the Toulon-bound ships. Once they were aboard, Nelson surrounded them with his fleet and refused to let them sail. It was a diabolical double-cross, on which Sir William reported gleefully to Acton back in Palermo in a couple of letters written immediately after the event. '... after good reflection, Lord Nelson authorised me to write to His Eminence this morning early, to certify to him that he would do nothing to break the armistice...' Sir William did not elaborate that Nelson's use of the word 'armistice' had been a deliberate trick, when the correct word to use would have been 'capitulation'. Sir William went on to tell Acton that Nelson had promised Ruffo any assistance the Republicans needed for their embarkation to Toulon. The following day he wrote again, exposing the shabby trick: 'Lord Nelson, concluding that his Sicilian Majesty has totally disapproved all that the Cardinal has done in contradiction to his instructions as regards the rebels of the castles, and those rebels being further on board twelve or fourteen transports ... Lord Nelson has believed himself sufficiently authorised to seize the transports and have them anchored in the middle of the British fleet ... I have reason to believe that ... we have all the greatest traitors on board . . . and that the *coup* will have been totally unexpected.'

The *coup*, if it could be called by such a name, was the work of Nelson and Sir William, and had nothing to do with Emma. Both men knew that if they were to survive, they must justify themselves by restoring Ferdinand to his throne and they were totally unscrupulous as to how they achieved their ends. To cover himself at home in England, Sir William for the first time in his career as an Ambassador sent home a grossly misleading account of the true course of events, and blamed any atrocities which followed squarely on the Neapolitan character.

For the moment, the prisoners aboard the transports were reasonably safe. But the unfortunates who had chosen to return to their homes suffered a fate which is remembered in Naples to this day. They were sought out by the *lazzaroni*, dragged from their houses into the streets, and butchered. Men, women and children were mutilated, used for target or bayonet practice, and when they could no longer stand, decapitated and their heads used as footballs. Not only Republicans suffered this fate, but anyone whom the mob took a dislike to, who had the short hair favoured by the Jacobins, or against whom the *lazzaroni* had old scores to settle. Contemporary accounts speak of piles of severed limbs standing on the street corners and of the *lazzaroni* roasting and eating human flesh; of women and children running a gauntlet down the quayside, while the *lazzaroni* stood in twin lines stabbing them as they ran to the apparent safety of the sea and the Toulon transports which they mistakenly believed offered a sanctuary. Those who escaped the mob were thrown into jail, there to await Ferdinand's pleasure.

While the mob wrought its own terrible vengeance, Prince Francesco Caracciolo was brought in chains to the *Foudroyant*, at which Sir William hurriedly penned a note to Acton that he expected to see him hanging from the yardarm by sunset; he was right for once. Nelson handed him over to a Neapolitan court martial, and on hearing the verdict of guilty, Nelson himself signed his rival's death warrant. He ordered the Neapolitan court martial:

'. . . You are hereby required and directed to cause the said sentence of death to be carried into execution upon the said Francesco Caracciolo accordingly, by hanging him at the yard forearm of his Sicilian Majesty's frigate *La Minerva*, under your command at five o'clock this evening; and to cause him to hang there until sunset, when you will have his body cut down, and thrown into the sea.'

Nelson

Given on board the *Foudroyant*, Naples Bay, 29 June 1799

Successive historians have claimed that Emma was at Nelson's side throughout this discreditable period and that she wilfully encouraged him to such excesses at the instigation of the Queen. This is palpably untrue, but such eminent historians and biographers as Southey, Allison and Brenton all made this mistake. They claim that Emma watched the execution with relish, and that late in the evening she insisted on being rowed around the ship to view the body. In order to evoke sympathy for the unfortunate Neapolitan Admiral, these earlier writers also made him out to be an old and broken man; in fact he was an active forty-seven, and he was also undoubtedly guilty of high treason. Emma did not in fact even see the execution, as she was dining with Lord Northwick at the time. She also had considerable sympathy for Caracciolo, as can be shown from correspondence between her and Maria Carolina, which though it has survived was not available to nineteenth-century historians.

The main reason why Emma has been accused of being the bloodthirsty agent of the Queen is the existence of a series of letters from Maria Carolina to Emma constantly urging her to tell Nelson to 'treat Naples as the English would an Irish town', or to make a 'severe example of some thousands' or, harsher still, 'we must have no regard for numbers, several thousand villains less will make France the poorer and we shall be better off!' However, there were other letters which said exactly the opposite, and which are written on the same dates. These counsel magnanimity, and many of them go to extraordinary lengths in persuading Emma to obtain pardons for many of the Jacobins. The reason for this paradox is simple. It was Ferdinand who wanted vengeance, and it was Ferdinand to whom Nelson was ultimately responsible. Ferdinand had joined Nelson in the Bay of Naples, leaving the Queen behind in Palermo, and was now on board the *Foudroyant*, which he used as a base, being too frightened to go ashore. The Queen's bellicose letters which she addressed to Emma were meant to be shown to the King; her gentler ones, for Emma's eyes only, came in envelopes addressed to Emma by her mother. These were pleas to Emma to persuade Nelson to rescue some of the less guilty prisoners aboard the transports, whom Ferdinand was executing in droves, his only stipulation being that the carnage should cease at noon each day so as not to interfere with his luncheon, or the drawing of the daily lottery.

Through Emma the Queen wrote to Nelson that she hoped everything could be settled without shedding blood: 'I still regard that ungrateful city and solicit your forebearance.' Later, after a successful plea for mercy for the brother of a friend, she wrote that she was convinced Emma and Nelson had saved his life. Indeed Nelson did spare many of those whom Emma pleaded for; Maria Carolina's letters of thanks have the postscript: 'I send this letter under your mother's envelope, and the other I write in order that it may be shown wholly...'

Glimpses of the Queen's replies to Emma's daily letters show us what the two women really thought about what was going on. Both are meant to have relished Caracciolo's death but it obviously offended Emma, for a surviving letter of Maria Carolina's reads: 'I have received with infinite gratitude your dear obliging letters, three of Saturday and one of anterior date bearing the list of Jacobins arrested... I have also noted the sad but merited end of the unfortunate crazy Caracciolo. I comprehend all that your excellent heart must have suffered and that augments my gratitude.' Then she referred to Emma's suggestion that mercy was a greater solace than vengeance, for she replied, 'I see perfectly what you point out to me, and am filled with gratitude for it.'

Meanwhile the executions continued. The nobility were beheaded but, by Ferdinand's command, they had to lie on their backs, eye unbandaged, so that they could see the axe. The middle classes were hanged, Neapolitan style; this involved the victims climbing up to a platform, having the noose placed around their necks and then being pushed off into space. The executioner would then jump on his victims' shoulders while his assistants hung on to the condemned persons' legs, in an attempt to pull off their heads. The monks of the Cathedral protested that the condemned were allowed no time to make their peace with God between sentence and execution, and that there was such a congestion of bodies in the main square that instead of being taken away for burial, they were being defiled and sometimes eaten by the mob. Meanwhile, Captain Troubridge was busy again. The French garrison had surrendered, and when they marched out, Troubridge discovered a number of Neapolitans who had been hiding with them in the fortress. He promptly set about them in his own fashion, reporting, 'I am really making the best I can out of the *degenerated race* I have to deal with. I have got a packed jury, Darby at their head, for fear justice should not reach the villains.' Nelson was treating Naples to a dose of the British naval discipline that had caused the mutinies at the Nore and Spithead; and to show he did not differentiate between Neapolitans and Englishmen he sentenced one of his own sailors, guilty of insubordination, to be hanged from the *Foudroyant*'s yardarm.

There was only one protest against the excesses of Ferdinand and Nelson, and that was a mute one. On the evening of 1 August Ferdinand was happily amusing himself shooting seagulls from the poop of the *Foudroyant* when he noticed what he thought was a dolphin in the water. He drew Sir William's attention to it, and playfully aimed his gun. Suddenly he realised it was no dolphin, but the body of Caracciolo which had broken free from the chains weighing it down and was now drifting slowly towards the *Foudroyant*, the head and shoulders standing clear out of the water. Ferdinand gibbered with terror, but Sir William saved the situation by suggesting that Caracciolo was merely coming to ask the Royal forgiveness and suggested that Ferdinand could make his peace by allowing him to have a Christian burial. To this Ferdinand agreed.

All references to the appalling scenes at Naples, and Nelson's opinion of them, are missing from his personal papers, and it is not surprising if he deleted them. The only reference he makes to what was going on during his short stay is in a letter to his wife dated 4 August. In this, he makes much of how Ferdinand and Maria Carolina depend on him, and appears much more interested in a party Ferdinand gave for him, to celebrate the first anniversary of the Battle of the Nile.

Naples 4 August 1799

'My Dear Fanny,—A few days ago brought me your letter of 6 May from Clifton, but since then I see by the papers you have been in London. I am glad you went to Court on the King's birthday... Thank God all goes well in Italy and the Kingdom of Naples is liberated from thieves and murderers, but still it has so overthrown the fabric of a regular government that much time and great care is necessary to keep the country quiet. Their Majesties have confidence in my counsels which they know to be disinterested and are fixed in the belief that whatever I undertake is sure of success and indeed this is general to the Kingdom. However flattering this may be, it has its alloys for if anything was to go wrong my popularity would be over.

The 1 August was celebrated here with as much respect as our situation would admit. The King dined with me and when His Majesty drank my health a Royal salute of twenty-one guns was fired from all HM's ships-of-war and from all the castles. In the evening there was a general illumination. Amongst others a large vessel was fitted out like a Roman galley. On the oars were fixed lamps and in the centre was erected a rostral column with my name, at the stern elevated were two angels supporting my picture. In short the beauty of the thing was beyond my powers of description. More than two thousand variegated lamps were fixed around the vessel, an orchestra was fitted up and filled with the very best musicians and singers. The piece of music was in a great measure my praises, describing their distress, but Nelson comes, the invincible Nelson and we are safe and happy again. Thus you must not make you think me vain [*sic*] so far very far from it and I relate it more from gratitude than vanity.

I return to Palermo with the King tomorrow and what may then be my movements it is impossible for me to say.

May God bless you all. My dear father must forgive my not writing so often as I ought and so must my brothers and friends but ever believe me your affectionate Nelson.' To Lady Nelson, Round Wood, Ipswich, Suffolk.

It was high time that Nelson left Naples, but his return to Palermo was quite unnecessary, apart from giving the King and the Hamiltons a passage back. Lord Keith, his new commander-in-chief who had succeeded St Vincent, had already cautioned him against any excesses at Naples. 'Advise those Neapolitans not to be too sanguinary, cowards are always cruel, give them fair words and a little confidence.' Nelson had ignored him. Keith then took a stronger line. He requested Nelson to assist him in the siege of Minorca, and when again Nelson ignored this request, Keith gave him a direct order to leave Naples and report to him off Minorca at once. Nelson, now so engrossed in Neapolitan affairs, and arrogant with power, refused to obey, writing to Keith that he considered the restoration of Naples of far more tactical importance than Minorca. He was probably right, but his attitude infuriated both Keith and the Admiralty. Privately he was censured, but gossip at Keith's headquarters at Gibraltar maintained that it was Emma who was holding him captive, and not his sense of duty to the Neapolitans. Lady

Elgin, the wife of the British Minister at Constantinople, wrote home from Gibraltar that, 'They say there never was a man turned so vain-glorious in the world as Lord Nelson. He is completely managed by Lady Hamilton.'

Hamilton's enemies at Palermo were also writing their spiteful letters, even though they had not been at Naples. Mr Lock, the Consul, who loathed Sir William and Emma, now included Nelson in his opprobrium. Nelson had caught him out in a petty swindle over supplies to the fleet, and he wrote to powerful relations at home that the sole blame for the horrors of Naples lay on the Queen and Emma, with Nelson as their willing tool. Nothing could have been further from the truth. All Emma had done was to send the Queen lists of the prisoners held either in the transports or the prisons, and between them they had rescued many from Ferdinand's vengeance. It was in this sphere and this sphere alone that the Queen and Emma used Nelson. Lock went further and told his London cronies that the fleet was near mutiny in disgust at the double-cross of the Republican prisoners, and that they regarded Emma as their Admiral's cruel and vindictive doxy.

This tittle-tattle began to find its way into the papers and satirical pamphlets of the time. Nelson was castigated for his vanity over his dress, but generally the satirists were gentle to him as a hero in love. Had not Anthony abandoned his campaign in Egypt for the lures of Cleopatra? There was nothing wrong in the hero of the Nile following such a distinguished precedent. It was poor Emma who became the butt of the more vicious jokes, and for the cruelty and dishonour of Naples Emma and the Queen bore the brunt of the public's disgust.

In Parliament, Charles James Fox tried to censure Nelson for his conduct, but his effort achieved very little success. England still needed its heroes, and the government preferred to believe Sir William's carefully emasculated reports of what had occurred. It was in this atmosphere, heavy with whispers and innuendoes, that Nelson brought the King and the Hamiltons back to

Palermo, and with petulant and obstinate pig-headedness ignored Lord Keith's orders and established his headquarters once again in the Hamiltons' house. His decision might well have been influenced by the reception that the Queen had prepared for them at Palermo. On his arrival, he remarked grandly to the Queen, 'Madam, I bring the present of a kingdom.' The Queen in turn showered everyone with presents. Emma was loaded in diamonds and two carriage loads of fine dresses to make up for the wardrobe she had left in Naples.

Sir William received a miniature of Ferdinand set in diamonds, and Nelson was granted the Dukedom of Bronte, a large Sicilian estate with an income in rents—if they could be collected—of £3,000 a year. The King gave 2,300 ounces of silver to be shared amongst the crew of the *Foudroyant*. Apart from the monetary gifts, the Royal Family showed their gratitude in a series of public gestures which bordered on idolatry to the *Tria Juncta in Uno*. First a celebratory mass was held in the vast Saracen Cathedral of Palermo with, after the *Te Deum*, a special cantata beginning 'Long live the British hero, Long Live great Nelson.' This was followed a few days later by a *fête champêtre* to commemorate the recovery of Naples. This *fête* and the festivities that followed it were the crowning follies which were to turn Nelson's head completely. The centrepiece of the party was a splendid Temple of Fame, built in Greco-classical style, dominated by three life-size wax statues of Nelson, Emma and Sir William. The figure of Nelson was decked with replicas of every award and honour that he had ever won, and a good few that he had not. Sir William's effigy was not so highly decorated, while Emma's was dressed to represent the Goddess of Victory, wearing a white silk robe and holding garlands of laurels in her hands.

The King, his Queen and their numerous children were all dressed in what they considered to be a 'nautical style', the Queen and the Princesses emblazoned with anchors and ribbons embroidered with Nelson's name. The Royal party stood on the steps of the temple to receive their guests, who had followed the Royal example in their dress, and when the guests had been received the *Tria Juncta in Uno* arrived to a fanfare of trumpets.

Sir William stood aside to let Emma go first, but an equerry signalled that Nelson should precede her. He approached the King, who after embracing him took a wreath of laurel from the wax Emma and crowned him with it amid tumultuous applause. Sir William and Emma were similarly crowned. This ceremony was followed by several hours of dancing, speech-making and odes sung in Nelson's honour, and then the entire party and their guests mounted a huge triumphal car seventy feet long, thirty feet wide and allegedly almost eighty feet high. This was dragged up and down the streets of Palermo by a team of sixty mules. The party went on for four days, every pageant, every spectacle making Nelson the idol of public adoration. The celebrations were brought to a climax with a spectacular firework display arranged by Ferdinand, which included the blowing up of a replica of the *Orient*.

Nelson was thrilled by it all and he persuaded Miss Cornelia Knight to write a description of the celebrations. Miss Knight, a sycophantic young woman, obliged, stressing the important part Nelson had played in the ceremonies and how beautiful Emma had looked. In an excess of vanity, Nelson sent it home to his brother Maurice with the request that it be inserted in *The Times*. In due course it appeared, doing nothing but harm to all concerned and enraging Nelson's wife. Most damaging of all, it appeared to confirm many of the nastier rumours that had begun to reach England.

However, many of these rumours were completely untrue. The gossips contended that during the seven months that the Hamiltons and Nelson had been in Naples there had been continuous rounds of parties and gambling sessions. Emma, they said, was losing £500 a night, and poor Nelson was being forced to finance the Hamiltons' profligate way of life. In fact Hamilton and Nelson shared all expenses, keeping scrupulous accounts. The truth is that both the Hamiltons and Nelson were far too busy for it to be possible for these rumours to be true. Lord Keith, who had gone out into the Atlantic to blockade Brest, had left Nelson as acting commander-in-chief of the Mediterranean and Nelson also had a busy headquarters staff to attend to. He was working every day from eight in the morning until eight at night, and during this period he also found the time to patrol in the *Foudroyant*, to spend a fortnight off Minorca, and to assist in the blockade of Malta. In his absence Emma acted as his confidential secretary, and nursed Sir William, who was seriously ill and past ambassadorial duties.

Emma and Nelson also had to try to keep the peace between the King and Queen, who had squabbled again and had settled at opposite sides of the city. The British Embassy was the only source of order and organisation in the tottering and extravagant edifice of government that Ferdinand had imposed. The King was in no hurry to return to Naples, and the Queen had but one wish and that was to leave Ferdinand and Italy for good and settle home in her beloved Vienna. It was British policy to maintain a friendly relationship with the Austrians, who were a far more useful ally than the Neapolitans, and therefore Nelson and Emma had to remain friends with the Queen, though still paying lip service to the idle and spendthrift King. Not infrequently they had to go behind the King's back. The affair of the corn from Malta is a typical example.

Nelson was blockading Malta. The French garrison had locked themselves up in Valetta and the islanders were desperately short of food. On a whim Ferdinand forbade the export of anything from either Naples or Sicily, although their granaries were bulging with corn. At Nelson's request Emma went to the Queen, obtaining two shiploads of corn which the Queen paid for, and the ships were covertly sent on their way to help feed the wretched Maltese. Emma was really extremely busy, and yet she still found time to write to Greville, and was actively working to find a job for her daughter, whom she had not seen for fourteen years, in the Queen's *entourage*. She was also extremely distressed at the rumours and innuendoes which the British papers were now openly stating. One said that Sir William had challenged Nelson to a duel over her, another that her wild gambling parties were sucking Nelson dry, and another that she was keeping him away from the fleet. In fact, with the exception of two periods of a fortnight's sick leave, Nelson was never under the Hamiltons' roof for longer than three days at a time.

By the spring, Nelson's ships had succeeded in capturing the last two French ships which had escaped at the Battle of the Nile. His mission was completed. He had totally annihilated the French fleet, he had restored Ferdinand to his throne, and now he asked for, and was given, permission to return home. Sir William also received his notice of recall, which was long overdue. He was now in his seventieth year, and there were many who doubted if he would survive the rigours of the journey home. Nelson, Emma and Sir William decided to go home together, but before they left they arranged to take a brief cruise together to Syracuse and Malta, keeping a safe distance from the Fortress of Valetta.

It was on this cruise that Nelson and Emma's affair started once more. Sir William had fallen down a staircase aboard the *Foudroyant*, Emma had been running a mild fever, and Nelson had had a minor heart attack. He decided to anchor at St Paul's Bay on the south side of Malta and for a week they rented a little house. While Sir William rested his bruises, Nelson and Emma stumbled again into the affair that the gossips were adamant had been going on for the past twelve months. Sir William was too intelligent not to have noticed by this time, but he kept his thoughts to himself, and anyway he was convinced that he had a very short time to live. Ideally he planned to return to England to settle his affairs and then return to Italy to die in the sunshine he loved. Privately, he doubted if he would live that long and even wrote to Greville giving arrangements about his funeral and burial place. Sir William knew it was time to leave the stage to Emma and Nelson, and he wished to do so as gracefully as possible.

The three of them dreaded going home. The more spiteful cartoons and articles in the English press had been sent out to them, and the two men at least knew what was awaiting them when they arrived in England. To delay that reckoning, they decided to travel overland. After a final farewell dinner party, they set sail with the Queen and her daughters to Leghorn, whence they planned to travel overland to Vienna, and from there to Hamburg and England. The party was a considerable one. The Queen, who was travelling with them as far as Vienna, had a suite of fifty people, Nelson's barge-crew travelled with the Hamiltons' baggage, and apart from the Hamiltons' servants there was Emma's mother and the effusive Miss Cornelia Knight, who had become a semi-permanent fixture in the household. This lady has left a series of letters which vividly describe the rigours of the journey. In her first she remarks that Sir William was convinced that he would die on the way, and these extracts from subsequent letters show that it was surprising that he did not.

July 24th 1800

'We left Leghorn the day after I wrote to you, and owing more to good fortune than to prudence, arrived in twenty-six hours at Florence, after passing within two miles of the French advance posts. After a short stay, we proceeded on our way to this place. At Castel San Giovanni, the coach, in which were Lord Nelson and Sir William and Lady Hamilton, was overturned; Sir William and Lady Hamilton were hurt, but not dangerously. The wheel was repaired, but broke again at Arezzo—the Queen two days' journey before them, and news of the French Army advancing rapidly, it was therefore decided that they should proceed, and Mrs Cadogan and I remained with the broken carriage, as it was of less consequence we should be left behind, or taken, than they. We were obliged to stay three days to get the coach repaired; and, providentially Arezzo was the place, as it is the most loyal city in Tuscany; and every care, attention, and kindness that humanity can dictate, and cordiality and good manners practise, were employed in our favour... Just as we were going to set off, we received accounts of the French being very near the road where we had to pass, and of its being also infested with Neapolitan deserters; but at the same moment arrived a party of Austrians, and the officers gave us two soldiers as a guard. We travelled night and day; the roads are almost destroyed, and the misery of the inhabitants is beyond description. At length, however, we arrived at Ancona, and found that the Queen had given up the idea of going in the *Bellona* an Austrian frigate, fitted up with silk hangings, carpets, and eighty beds for her reception, and now meant to go with a Russian squadron of three frigates and a brig. I believe she judged rightly; for there had been a mutiny on board the *Bellona*, and, for the sake of accommodation, she had reduced her guns to twenty-four, while the French, in possession of the coast, arm *trabaccoli* and other light vessels that could easily surround and take her. Mrs Cadogan and I are to be on board one of the frigates, commanded by an old man named Messer, a native of England, who once served under Lord Howe, and has an excellent reputation. The rest of the party go with the Queen, and say they shall be very uncomfortable.'

Trieste, 9 August 1800

'I told you we were become humble enough to rejoice at a Russian squadron conveying us across the Adriatic; but had we sailed, as we first intended, in the imperial frigate, we should have been taken by eight *trabaccoli*, which the French armed on purpose at Pisaro. Sir William and Lady Hamilton and Lord Nelson gave a miserable account of their sufferings on board the commodore's ship (Count Voinovitsch). He was ill in his cot; but his first lieutenant, a Neapolitan named Capaci, was, it seems, the most insolent and ignorant of beings. Think what Lord Nelson must have felt! He says a gale of wind would have sunk the ship. I, with Mrs Cadogan, came in another ship, commanded, as I believe I told you, by an Englishman, a Captain Messer, a plain, good man, who behaved with distinguished bravery last year at the siege of Ancona, and who was kind and attentive beyond description... Poor Sir William Hamilton has been so ill that the physicians had almost given him up: he is now better, and I hope we shall be able to set off tomorrow night for Vienna. The Queen and thirty-four of her suite have had fevers: you can form no idea of the helplessness of the party. How we shall proceed on our long journey is to me a problem; but we shall certainly get on as fast as we can; for the very precarious state of Sir William's health has convinced everybody that it is necessary he should arrange his affairs...'

Vienna, 30 August 1800

'Lord Nelson arrived here with Sir W. and Lady Hamilton a few days after the Queen of Naples, having been detained at Trieste some time by Sir William's illness. Sir W. has had a relapse here; and altho' he has recovered a little yet he is so feeble and so much reduced that I cannot see how it is possible for him to reach England alive. Lord Nelson has been received here by all ranks with the admiration which his great actions deserve, and notwithstanding the disadvantage under which he presents himself at present to the public eye. They talk of proceeding in a few days towards England; and I who am a lover of naval merit and indeed a sincere friend of the man, hope we shall again hear of him on his proper element...'

Sir William was seriously ill in Vienna, and the journey home was delayed for six weeks while he recovered his strength. Meanwhile Nelson and Emma were fêted everywhere, the Viennese recognising and approving of their now very obvious love for each other. Eventually, Sir William recovered; the three of them said their goodbyes to Queen Maria Carolina and travelled in easy stages by way of Prague, Dresden and Hamburg to the port of Cuxhaven where they waited for a ship to England.

Everywhere they had been royally entertained, but their journey was slower than the posts, and letters describing their appearance and behaviour preceded them. Most were unflattering: there were spiteful reports that Nelson was drinking too much champagne, boasting, and clamouring for songs and toasts in his honour; and there were sarcastic jibes at Emma's accent and her exceptionally large though still well-proportioned figure. Nelson was regarded as as much of a parvenu as Emma, for he had neither the bearing nor the presence to wear so many decorations without looking ridiculous. 'Lord Nelson is a little man without any dignity.' 'She is without exception the most coarse, ill-mannered woman I have ever met with.' At Cuxhaven they secured berths on the mail packet the *King George* and landed at Great Yarmouth, after an exceptionally rough crossing, on 6 November 1800. Here they were given a hero's welcome, for the ordinary people were not concerned with social shortcomings. Nelson was their idea of a hero, with his empty sleeve and heavy lidded eye, and Emma was still a beautiful woman. Three days later they arrived in London during a heavy thunderstorm, and Nelson was reunited with his wife at Nerot's Hotel in King Street, St James. It cannot have been a very cheerful meeting, for that morning a pamphlet had been on sale in the street outside, which parodied the National Anthem.

> Also huge Emma's name
> First on the role of fame,
> and let us sing.
> Loud as her voice, let's sound
> Her faded charms around
> Which in the sheets were found,
>   God save the King.
>
> Nelson, thy flag haul down,
> Hang up thy laurel crown,
>   While her we sing.
> No more in triumph swell,
> Since that with her you dwell,
> But don't her William tell—
> Nor George, your King.

IX

November 1800–October 1801

Two
Blind Eyes

'Now, my own dear wife, for such
you are in my eyes and in the face of
heaven ... there is nothing in this
world that I would not do for us to
live together, and to have our dear
little child with us.'

Nelson to Emma before the
Battle of Copenhagen

The newspapers had a field day, and for a day or two were
kind to Emma. The *Morning Post* reported:

'His Lordship arrived yesterday afternoon at three
o'clock at Nerot's Hotel, King Street, St James, in the
German travelling carriage of Sir William Hamilton. In the
coach came with his Lordship Sir William and Lady
Hamilton... The noble Admiral who was dressed in full
uniform, with three stars on his breast and two gold
medals, was welcomed with repeated hurras from the
crowd which the illustrious tar returned with a low bow.
Lord Nelson looked extremely well but in person is very
thin: so is Sir William: but Lady Hamilton looks
charmingly, and is a very fine woman... about ten
minutes after their arrival his Grace the Duke of
Queensberry paid them a visit... At five o'clock Lord
and Lady Nelson, Sir William and Lady Hamilton dined
together. At half past seven his Lordship... went to Lord

Spencer, and about half an hour later, Lady Nelson paid a friendly visit to the Countess Spencer, where with a select company they passed the evening.'

The dinner had been a frigid one, with Fanny Nelson coldly eyeing Emma, realising from her size that this time she was well and truly pregnant; she would not have been human if she had not wondered who was the father. After dinner when Nelson had left for his interview, the Hamiltons moved up the street to Grosvenor Square where Sir William's young cousin, William Beckford, had lent them his London house until they could find somewhere to live. Waiting for them was a note from Charles Greville which hinted that neither the Court nor the Foreign Office would be particularly pleased to see any of them, and that rumours of the atrocities at Naples and of their strange *ménage à trois* had preceded them. Greville was quite adamant that although Emma carried a letter of introduction from the Queen of Naples to the Queen of England, she would not be received at Court. Nevertheless, the Hamiltons determined to brazen it out. They had their own friends, and so far their reception had been as tumultuous from the populace as it had been frigid from polite society.

This needs qualifying. Polite society did not include such people as the Prince of Wales, or his equally profligate brothers, the Dukes of Clarence and Sussex. They were accepted everywhere because of their birth, as was the Duke of Queensberry, although he was one of the most disgusting old reprobates in the Kingdom, known to everyone as 'Old Q'. The polite society who were to ostracize the Hamiltons were the men whose wives had been presented to Queen Charlotte, herself an incredibly stuffy woman. Sir William reckoned he could do without this form of social accolade, but insisted that they remain in London, where it was possible that Nelson's presence and constant company considerably strengthened his own popularity and personal resolve. Once the news was out that Emma was not to be received at Court, the newspapers began to mock her. First, there were cheap little jibes at her figure. The *Morning Herald* led off, spitefully exaggerating her age.

'Her Ladyship is in her forty-ninth year, rather taller than the common height, still displaying a superior graceful animation of figure, now a little on the wane, from too great a propensity to the *en bon point*. Her attitudinarian graces, so varying in their style, and captivating in their effect, are declining also, under this unfortunate personal extension. Her teeth are lovely, and her hair is of the darkest brown, immensely thick, and trails to the ground. Her eyes are black, and possess the most fascinating attraction, but her nose is rather too short for the Grecian contour of her face, which, notwithstanding, is singularly expressive; and her conversazioni, if not solid and argumentative, are at least sprightly and unceasing. Such, after ransacking Herculaneum and Pompeii, for thirty-eight years, is the chief curiosity with which that celebrated antiquarian Sir William Hamilton, has returned to his native country.'

The *Post*, picking up this reference to Emma's 'unfortunate personal extension', remarked that 'Lady Hamilton was fitting up a room for the purpose of displaying her attitudes and in a short time will give large attitude parties. *Attitudes* it is thought will be much more in vogue this winter than *shape or feature.*' The *Times* was blunter than most. 'Lady Hamilton has arrived in the very nick of time in this country.' Soon scurrilous little articles relating her activities at Doctor Graham's as the Goddess of Health were a commonplace in almost every scandal sheet on sale in the city.

Nelson spent as much time as possible with the Hamiltons, using the Grosvenor Square house whenever he wished to entertain, which was almost every evening. He too decided to brazen the matter out, and he too had been publicly snubbed by no less a person than the King. Two days after he arrived he had attended the *levée* at St

James, and after being presented to the King, who had enquired briefly as to his health, had to stand helpless as the King turned his back on him without waiting for his answer and spoke for half an hour to some undistinguished officer before giving Nelson a cursory nod that he might withdraw. This was a public humiliation with a vengeance, and seeking a chance to work off his spleen Nelson took his revenge on the wretched Fanny. That evening at dinner he was so cold to her that she burst into tears and rushed from the room. Countess Spencer who was present noted that 'he treated her with every mark of dislike, and even of contempt'. However, despite his coldness, he insisted that Fanny accompany him whenever he went out publicly with the Hamiltons. The spectacle cannot have been a pretty one, and eventually it came to a climax in a scene of dramatic irony.

Every night after dinner the four of them had gone to the theatre. On each occasion the audience had risen to applaud Nelson in his box, and this adulation must have been the only solace the vain Nelson was to have. The *Morning Post* described his reception at the Theatre Royal in the Haymarket: 'The whole audience rose to salute him in an ecstasy of joy, clapping, hurraying and waving their hats. His Lordship seemed much affected; and never was enthusiasm more warm and more prolonged than that with which he was received.' This nightly tonic came to an abrupt end when on 24 November Nelson and Sir William took their wives, together with Nelson's father the Reverend Edmund, to Drury Lane to see a somewhat lurid melodrama called *Pizarro*, which Sheridan had rescued from its author, Kotzebue, and brightened up with his own dialogue.

The plot centres on the heroine, Elvira, who pleads with her lover Pizarro for the life of another lover called Alonzo. Pizarro refuses her entreaties, and towards the *finale* announces, 'Alonzo dies at dawn'; walking off the stage to leave Elvira to bring down the house with a massively emotional speech. The speech is full-blooded eighteenth-century melodrama, and that night there was a packed house, as word had got out that the Nelsons were to attend. When they entered their box, the audience rose to its feet and sang *Rule Britannia*. Then a hush as the play began. Emma was surprised on consulting her programme to find that Mrs Siddons was not playing the heroine, as had been advertised. She was indisposed, and in her place was an old friend of Emma's from her days with Dr Budd in Blackfriars, Jane Powell. Suspecting nothing, Emma settled down to enjoy both the play and the pleasure of seeing her friend again.

When the curtain lifted, the audience gasped, for the plot was set in Naples and the management of Drury Lane had gone to enormous expense to create a backdrop in which Vesuvius had been given a real crater which intermittently belched smoke and thunder. The melodrama wound its way through three acts, until the time came when Pizarro stalked off the stage, leaving Elvira to make her closing speech. This time Jane Powell, instead of kneeling and gazing after the departing figure, came to the front of the stage immediately below Nelson's box. Gradually, while the volcano flickered with a red glow, she whipped the audience up to a histrionic frenzy as she declaimed through tears: 'Fall fall, ye few reluctant drops of weakness—the last these eyes shall ever shed. How a woman can love, Pizarro, thou hast known too well—how she can hate, thou hast yet to learn. Yes thou undaunted! ... thou who braved the raging elements ... the crashing thunder ... the red volcano's mouth! Thou who when battling on the sea bestrode a fragment of the smoking wreck ... waving thy sword above thy head as thou wouldst defy the world...' She paused and flung her arm up towards Nelson, before delivering her closing lines: 'Come fearless man, now meet the last and fellest peril of thy life; meet and survive—an injured woman's fury if thou canst!'

In the silence as the curtain fell, while the audience was recovering its breath before applauding, there was a loud shriek from the box and Lady Nelson collapsed. She recovered quickly, helped by Emma and Nelson's father, but there was no applause from the audience. Nelson and

Hamilton sat alone together, speechless at the irony of the play and bitterly conscious of the electric atmosphere around them. Then slowly they rejoined the women and left the theatre. It was the last time Nelson and Fanny were ever seen together in public.

Nelson had other worries besides his marriage. He was very short of money. He had only his pay, and savings of about £8,000 which brought in an extra £400 a year. Of this he set aside £4,000 to invest for Fanny, as it was now obvious to him that they were going to have to separate. He spent the next week or two in London, trying to rationalise his affairs, and it was this shortage of funds, and the realisation that London was hateful to him, that prompted him to present himself at the Admiralty and ask to be sent to sea again. There at least he could save, until matters resolved themselves, for he did have some financial expectations. Between them, the Admiralty and Earl St Vincent owed him £14,000 in prize money, though he would have to go to law to get it. And Sir William owed him a little over £2,000, as part of his share of the expenses on the journey home, but Sir William, too, was financially embarrassed.

Sir William had an excellent case for compensation from the government. He had lost three houses and many of their contents to the French and the mob in Naples. He had had to carry the expenses of the British Embassy in Palermo entirely by himself, as the previous Foreign Secretary had omitted to pass on his claims, and Lord Hawkesbury, the present holder of that office, had neither the time nor the inclination to remedy the matter. Then Sir William had lost many of the items he had hoped to sell in the wreck of the *Colossus*, and the Treasury had not yet found the time to decide either how much of a pension he was going to have, or when to start paying it. He had no house, no furniture, except a few crates of nick-nacks he had brought from Palermo, and nowhere either to store or hang those of the pictures and vases which had arrived safely and upon which there were heavy charges for freight to be paid before he could collect them. All he had was the income from his late wife's Welsh estate, and that was heavily mortgaged.

Nelson sat down with him, and the two men desperately tried to work out and present his claim on the Treasury. Between them they calculated what he was owed. Eventually he claimed £13,213 in arrears of salary and expenses, and £10,000 for the loss of his property. The Treasury procrastinated and in fact Sir William never did receive a penny. However, while he lived he had hopes that he would be paid, and in the meantime he thankfully accepted a pension of £1,200 a year which was to cease at his death. This was a calculated insult to Emma from those in authority, and Sir William did not have the courage to tell her of its cessation when he died.

Emma helped him out of his immediate embarrassment. Hamilton insisted on living in London, so Emma sold her jewellery, including the diamonds that the Queen of Naples had given her, and with this money they took a long lease on a house at 23 Piccadilly, almost opposite the Royal Society's rooms. There was still more than enough money left to furnish it down to the last piece of linen or tableware. The lease, of course, was in Sir William's name, but he took care that his will stipulated that the contents were Emma's. However, once this capital was spent, neither Emma nor her husband had sufficient income to live the sort of life to which they had become accustomed over the last fifteen years. Either Sir William was going to have to sell some of his pictures and vases, or he would have to do what Emma would dearly have liked, and settle somewhere in the country—not too far from London. Suddenly out of the blue came a bizarre message from Sir William's young cousin, William Beckford.

Beckford was a curious amalgam of a man. He was gloomy, sensitive, artistic, yet capable of extreme banality. He it was who wrote the famous oriental fantasy *Vathek*. He was also one of the richest men in England, with an income of £300,000 a year from his family sugar estates in the West Indies, and a further £2 million invested in government securities. He would probably have bought his way into political power, but unfortunately he had been caught in a homosexual relationship with the young son of Viscount Courtenay, about the time that Emma first went to Naples. As a result he had lived abroad for a period until his disgrace had been forgotten and now lived at Fonthill in Wiltshire where he was building himself a vast Gothic abbey as a consolation for what might have been. However he was not content to indulge in architectural extravaganzas without having the social standing of one who was used to living in them. Beckford wished to be a duke, or at the very least a baron. He conceived the idea that possibly Hamilton could help him and wrote suggesting that Hamilton should apply for a peerage as his reward for being an ambassador for thirty-seven years, and that, as this could hardly be refused, Hamilton could name Beckford as his heir. In return, Beckford suggested that he paid Hamilton £2,000 a year while he lived, and on his death he would pay Emma a pension of £500 a year. Hamilton jumped at the offer, which was sufficiently Neapolitan to attract him. To cement the agreement, Beckford invited Emma and Sir William to spend Christmas with him; pragmatically he asked Nelson along as well. All three accepted, delighted to get out of London where their social ostracism was becoming more than either of the two men could bear. Fanny Nelson stayed behind to face a lonely Christmas in the furnished rooms that she and Nelson had taken.

Beckford had decided to make up a mammoth party for the occasion. His abbey was nearing completion, and he was anxious to show it off. He invited several members of the Royal Society, and a motley collection of sycophants, writers and artists. To please Emma, the famous Italian opera singer Madame Banti was included in the party. The *Tria Juncta in Uno*, united once more, set off for Wiltshire in Sir William's carriage, Sir William apparently much fitter than he had been for months, Emma eight months pregnant, and Nelson the centre of attention whenever he was recognised along the way; as he was quite unmistakable, and insisted on travelling in full uniform, this was in almost every hamlet, while places such as Salisbury insisted on giving him a civic reception and the Freedom of the City. Their arrival at Fonthill provided a taste of what was to come; Beckford had his own private army, 'The Fonthill Volunteers', dressed in a full-dress uniform of his own design, drawn up to meet them, and a band on the steps of his house playing *Rule Britannia*.

For six days they ate, sang and plotted. Beckford now had an even stranger plan, suggesting that somehow Hamilton, with Nelson's assistance, could get himself made the heir of Hamilton's eldest brother, the Duke of Hamilton, with whom neither Sir William nor the Admiral were on speaking terms. The pension of a dowager duchess, Beckford told Emma, would be far more than that of a bereaved peeress. Neither the Hamiltons nor Nelson took all this plotting very seriously. Sir William certainly made a few enquiries around the Court, but he was to die before anything concrete had been arranged. In the meantime, Beckford was providing them all with a welcome respite from reality. Just how different their host's way of life was from the everyday world was shown on the evening of 23 December. In a race against time he had had seven hundred workmen putting the finishing touches to his architectural folly, and during the afternoon it was announced that in the evening a surprising *divertissement* was in store. At five pm the guests came to the front door, where the 'Fonthill Volunteers' were waiting with a convoy of decorated carriages. One guest wrote an account of what happened in the *Gentleman's Magazine*:

'At a particular turn every carriage stopped and one long, loud, ringing shout of amazement and delight burst from every throat. The enormous body of visitors found themselves in an instant transported as by magic to a fairy scene. Through the far-stretching woods of pine glittered myriad on myriad of variegated lamps forming vast vistas of light defining the distant perspective as clearly as in sunshine. Flambeaux in profusion were carried about by bearers stationed wherever they were most needed. The Volunteers, handsomely accoutred, were drawn up on either side. Bands of music, studiously kept out of sight, were placed at intervals along the route, playing inspiring marches, the whole effect being heightened by the deep roll of numerous drums, so placed in the hollows of the hills as to ensure their reverberations being heard on every side. The profound darkness of the night, the many tinted lamps—some in motion, others stationary, here reflected on the bayonets and helmets of the soldiery, here seen through coloured glass, and so arranged as to shed rainbow hues on every surrounding object—the music, now with a dying fall, now waking the dormant echoes into life with marshalled clangour, riveted to the spot the lover of striking contrasts.

Gradually the procession drew near to the abbey itself, the tracery of its splendid architecture relieved by strong shadows, the inequalities of the building marked out by myriads of lights, and revealing, to the wondering eyes of the spectators, battlements and turrets and flying buttresses. No grander feature was there in the whole edifice than the tower shooting up three hundred feet, the upper part lost in total eclipse. Reared above the main entrance fluttered the national banner, and by its side the Admiral's flag, catching light enough as they flapped in the night breezes to display their massive folds to advantage.

All present stood entranced. The moment the abbey was fully disclosed, everyone, animated by a common impulse, sprang from his carriage and walked towards it; when the 'conquering hero' attended by his host entered the walls, the organ thundered forth a resounding peal of welcome, which shook the edifice to its foundations; while notes of triumph resounded from galleries and corridors around.

From the abbey they adjourned to the Grand Hall, which had been arranged for the banquet. An entire service of silver and agate of medieval pattern was laden with the fare of other days. On the board, and against the walls of the room, stood candles six feet high in silver sconces, while huge blazing logs of cedar, dried and prepared for the occasion, and continuously renewed, contributed to the material comfort.

The banquet ended and the guests, well-nigh surfeited with the fanciful and gorgeous display they had witnessed, were desired to pass up the grand staircase. On each side of it stood, at intervals, men dressed as monks, carrying waxen flambeaux in their hands. The company were first ushered into a suite of sumptuous apartments hung with gold-coloured satin damask, in which were ebony cabinets of inestimable value, inlaid with precious stones and filled with treasures collected from many lands—then through a gallery two hundred and eighty-five feet long into the library which was filled with choice books and rare manuscripts, and fitted up with consummate taste, the hangings of crimson velvet embroidered with arabesques of gold, the carpets of the same colour—the windows of old stained-glass bordered with the most graceful designs.

At last the guests reached the oratory, where a lamp of gold was burning by itself, shedding just light enough to display to advantage in a niche, studded with mosaics and jewels of great price, a statue of St Anthony by Rossi. Here again the illusion of the monastery was well maintained. Large candelabra, in stands of ebony inlaid with gold and multiplied by huge pier-glasses, formed an exquisite perspective and enhanced the surpassing brilliancy of the scene.

After the scenic representation, a collation was presented in the library, consisting of various sorts of confectionery served in gold baskets, with spiced wines, etc., whilst rows of chairs were placed in the great room beyond, which had first received the company above stairs. A large vacant place was left in front of the seats. The assembly had no sooner occupied them than Lady Hamilton appeared in the character of Agrippina, bearing the ashes of Germanicus in a golden urn, as she presented them before the Roman people, with the design of exciting them to revenge the death of her husband, who, after having been declared joint Emperor by Tiberius, fell a victim to his envy, and is supposed to have been poisoned by his order, at the head of the forces which he was leading against the rebellious Armenians. Lady Hamilton displayed with truth and energy every gesture, attitude, and expression of countenance which could be conceived in Agrippina herself, best calculated to have moved the passions of the Romans on behalf of their favourite general. The action of her head, of her hands, and arms in the various positions of the urn; in her manner of presenting it before the Romans, or of holding it up to the Gods in the act of supplication, was most classically graceful. Every change of dress, principally of the head, to suit the different situations in which she successively presented herself, was performed instantaneously with the most perfect ease, and without retiring or scarcely turning aside a moment from the spectators. In the last scene of this most beautiful piece of pantomime, she appeared with a young lady of the company, who was to impersonate a daughter. Her action in this part was so perfectly just and natural, and so pathetically addressed to the spectators as to draw tears from several of the company. It may be questioned whether this scene, without theatrical assistance of other characters and appropriate circumstances, could possibly be represented with more effect.

It was long after midnight before the visitors could tear themselves away. But their host would not permit them to linger in case they should retire with their impressions impaired by familiarity. So that, before the lamps began to wane, several bands, accompanied by the mighty organ, struck up their most exhilarating airs, and as these yet hung upon the ear of the departing guests, the night breeze wafting their melodies through the air till distance drowned it, they left the abbey grounds scarce able to believe that they had not been enjoying an Arabian night's entertainment instead of an English one.'

The return to London and normality was harsh. Nelson went back to Fanny's apartment, and learnt that he had been promoted Vice-Admiral of the Blue and was to be the second-in-command of an expedition which was to sail for the Baltic within the next two months. His time was fully occupied with packing his effects, briefings at the Admiralty, and squabbling with Fanny. The row which had been smouldering for months broke out into the open on 12 January, when Fanny asked him to choose between Lady Hamilton and herself, and then walked out. Nelson was glad it had happened at last, but it brought even more social ostracism upon him, and he wrote to Emma and Sir William: 'I find this world is full of jealousy and envy ... I see a faint gleam of future comfort ... I shall come to Grosvenor Square on my return ... and hope to find in the smiles of my friends some alleviation from the cold looks and cruel words of my enemies.'

The Hamiltons had in fact left Grosvenor Square, moving into 23 Piccadilly in early January. About three weeks later, probably on 28 January, Emma gave birth to Nelson's child, a girl whom she called Horatia. Much has been made of the fact that Emma concealed her pregnancy from society and from her husband. In fact to do so would have been, and has been described as, miraculous. The truth is that almost everyone was fully aware of her pregnancy. Sir William certainly was. However, the cardinal sin in Sir William's eyes was to offend against what society at the time called 'bienséance'. Basically this meant that it did not matter what happened as long as one did not make a fool of oneself or any one else in public. As long as the outward proprieties were observed, then extra-mural marital activities were cheerfully tolerated. All Sir William wished was that Emma would not publish her pregnancy and that she would arrange matters so that he suffered neither ridicule nor expense. This was a period which his contemporaries called the Age of Enlightenment, and Sir William was quite prepared to teach Nelson the art of turning a blind eye.

Emma did not let him down. The baby stayed in the house for a few days, and on the evening of 7 February Sir William arranged to dine out with the Duke of Sussex, announcing that Emma had a recurrence of their Italian bilious attacks. Shortly after he left, Emma took the baby to a wet nurse called Miss Gibson in Little Titchfield Street whom her mother, Mrs Cadogan, had tactfully organised. From now on, Nelson and Sir William were both busy arranging their affairs. Sir William was planning the sale of his pictures and vase collection, living an increasingly bachelor life among his clubs and his cronies at the Royal Society and Mr Christie's auction rooms. Occasionally he travelled to visit relations, but now he travelled alone. Nelson, busy off the south coast organising the Baltic expedition, rarely found time to come to London. He made a couple of hurried visits, to play with Horatia at Miss Gibson's or attend conferences at the Admiralty, and for propriety's sake he stayed in a nearby hotel while he lunched with naval friends and dined at 23 Piccadilly with the Hamiltons. He also visited his solicitors and arranged to make Fanny an allowance of half his pay, pending a formal deed of separation. The three of them wrote regularly to each other, and each in his own way thought that an embarrassing and delicate matter had been arranged very well.

Nelson's letters to Emma fall into three categories. There were those he wrote directly to her, which dealt with everyday subjects and which could be read by prying eyes at the Post Office without compromising anybody. Then there were the personal letters, frequently love letters, which he sent by trusted private hands. Occasionally, when no such courier was available, he invented a little subterfuge. He pretended that on board his ship he had a young *protégé* called Thompson. This imaginary character had a mistress with a small baby who was employed by Lady Hamilton in her household. With the aid of this fiction Nelson could work off his daily quota of protestations of love without fear of the existence of his and Emma's child being known to the public.

While Sir William was planning to sell his pictures, he unwittingly gave Nelson cause for morbid jealousy. Before the sale, he hung the pictures at 23 Piccadilly, inviting the connoisseurs he knew to view them. He was particularly keen to have the Prince of Wales attend the sale, and to whet his appetite invited him to dinner for a private view and to hear Emma sing. The Prince, who was far more interested in Emma than in art, let it be known that he would be delighted to accept as soon as he could find the time. To tempt him further, Sir William included in the sale Romney's portrait of Emma as St Cecilia. This was one of Nelson's favourite portraits, and when Sir William wrote, artlessly telling him of his plans, Nelson nearly went mad, taking offence at Sir William's remark that if the Prince did come, then the 'Emma' would sell for a better price.

The Prince of Wales was a notorious rake, and it could be said with a degree of truth that a woman who entertained him in her house usually finished up in bed with him, for it was considered grossly impolite for either the woman or her husband to stand in the way of the Royal inclination. Alone in his cabin, Nelson credited Sir William with the role of a pimp in an effort to better both his pocket and his waning popularity. A stinging series of letters to Emma were rushed off from wherever his flagship happened to be.

'I do not think I ever was so miserable as at this moment. I own I sometimes fear that you will not be so true to me as I am to you, yet I cannot, will not believe you can be false. No, I judge you by myself; I hope to be dead before that should happen, but it will not. Forgive me, Emma oh, forgive your own dear, disinterested Nelson. I cannot express my feelings. May God send me happiness. I have a letter from Sir William; he speaks of the Regency as certain, and then probably he thinks you will sell better—horrid thought. Only believe me for ever your, etc.'

Another letter followed this outburst the following day.

St George, 19 February 1801
'Forgive my letter wrote and sent last night, perhaps my head was a little affected. No wonder, it was such an unexpected, such a knockdown blow, such a death. But I will not go on, for I shall get out of my senses again. Will

you sing for the fellow, the Prince, unable to Conceal His
Pain, etc? No, you will not. I will say no more for fear of
my head. It was so good of you to send to thank Mr Nisbet
for his not asking you to meet the fellow, as he knew his
vile intent, and yet, the same morning to let him come and
dine with you *en famille*!—but I know it was not my
Emma; Sir William always asks all parties to dinner. I
forgive you. Forgive, I beseech, your old and dear friend!
Tell me all, every word, that passes. He will propose if
you—no, you will not try; he is Sir William's guest.

Thursday.—I have just got your letter, and I live again.
DO NOT let the lyar come. I never saw him but once, the 4th
day after I came to London, and he never mentioned your
name. May God Blast him! Be firm! Go and dine with Mrs
Denis on Sunday. Do not, I beseech you, risk being at
home. Does Sir William want you to be a whore to the
rascal? Forgive all my letter; you will see what I feel, and
have felt. I have eat not a morsel, except a little rice, since
yesterday morning, and till I know how this matter is gone
off. But I feel confident of your resolution and thank you
1,000,000 of times. I wrote you a letter, which may be said
as coming from me if you like, I will endeavour to word it
properly. Did you sit alone with the villain for a moment?
No, I will not believe it! Oh, God! oh, God! keep my
senses. Do not let the rascal in. Tell the duke that you will
never go to his house. Mr G. must be a scoundrel; he
treated you once ill enough, and cannot love you, or he
would sooner die. Ever for ever, aye for ever, your, etc.'

'How Sir William can associate with a person of a
character so diametrically opposite to his own, but I do not
choose, as this letter goes through many hands, to enter
more at large on this subject, I glory in your conduct and in
your inestimable friendship, and good Sir William, when
he reflects, must admire your virtuous and proper conduct.
I wish you were my sister, that I might instantly give you
half my fortune for your glorious conduct. Be firm! Your
cause is that of honour against infamy. May the Heavens
bless you, and let no consideration suffer you to alter your

virtuous and sensible resolution. Pardon all this from an old and interested friend. You know I would not in Sir William's case have gone to Court without my wife, and such a wife, never to be matched. It is true you would grace a Court better as a Queen than a visitor.

I again, my dear friend, entreat both you and Sir William not to suffer the Prince to dine, or even visit. 'Tis what no real modest person would suffer, and Sir William ought to know that his views are dishonourable. May God bless you and make you firm in resisting this vile attempt on your character. Your letters are just come. Heavens bless you! Do not let the villain into your house. Dine out on Sunday. Sir William will find out the Prince does not come to dine with him.'

After asking Emma to dine out and snub the Prince, Nelson must have realised that this would infuriate Sir William, for his precious '*bienséance*' would be affected and possibly he might throw Emma out. Immediately a 'Thompson' letter was sent.

'... Your most dear friend (Thompson) desires me to say that he sincerely feels for you, and that if your uncle is so hard-hearted as to oblige you to quit his house, he will instantly quit all the world and its greatness to live with you a domestic quiet life...'

Emma's reply must have reassured him for his next letter was not so hysterical.

'I have received your most affectionate letter, and I feel very much for the unpleasant situation the Prince, or rather Sir William, has unknowingly placed you, for if he knew as much of the P's character as the world does, he would rather let the lowest wretch that walks the streets dine at his table than the unprincipled lyar. I have heard it reported that he has said he would make you his mistress. Sir William never can admit him into his house, nor can any friend advise him to it unless they are determined on your hitherto unimpeached character being ruined. No modest woman would suffer it. He is permitted to visit only

houses of notorious ill fame. For heaven's sake let Sir
William pause before he damns your good name. Mr
Greville I take to be a man of strict honour, and he knows
what I say of the Prince to be true. If I have not mistaken
my man, which I shall be truly sorry to have done, I will
answer with my head that Mr Greville would go down on
his knees and beg Sir William to save your unspotted
honour, for although I know you would send him to the
Devil were he to propose such a thing to you, yet all the
world have their eyes upon you, and your character, my
amiable friend, is as much lost as if you was guilty. Let Sir
William consult any man of honour, and with readiness
they will join me in opinion. Let Sir William write the
Prince and say that you ought not to receive him, and beg
him never to come to the house—it is what I would do, I
give you my word of honour. I am sure the Duke of
Queensberry would agree with me. I have, my dear friend,
perhaps, given too full an opinion, but you know, when I
do give an opinion, it is generally to be understood, and,
hitherto, seldom wrong. Make my affectionate regards to
Sir William, and entreat him not to suffer such bad
company into his house, and do you and him ever believe
me your most attached and affectionate friend, etc.'

Emma and circumstances stopped the charade. She
developed a series of blinding headaches which eventually
cooled the Prince's ardour, and Nelson left with the fleet
under Captain Sir Hyde Parker for the Baltic and the Battle
of Copenhagen. Before he left he sent an open bid to Mr
Christie and managed to buy the portrait of Emma for
£300. It was a steep price in a sale where six studies by
Leonardo da Vinci only made £30. Perhaps Sir William's
plan had succeeded after all.

Before he left, Nelson wrote one letter to Emma which
he sent by a Mr Oliver, a close friend of both the
Hamiltons and himself, who was aware of the true state of
affairs. Both Sir William and Nelson used Oliver as a
secretary, and he lived in the Hamilton household. This
letter has been described as probably the most important

Nelson ever wrote. That may be right, for it certainly clears away all the doubts that later biographers cast on Horatia's parentage in an effort to burnish Nelson's image at Emma's expense. In it, he plans to make a formal separation from Fanny and as soon as Sir William dies, to escape to his Sicilian estate to live happily ever after. It was a lovely dream for him to take to battle.

'Now, my own dear wife, for such you are in my eyes and in the face of heaven, I can give full scope to my feelings, for I dare say Oliver will faithfully deliver this letter. You know, my dearest Emma, that there is nothing in this world that I would not do for us to live together, and to have our dear little child with us. I firmly believe that this campaign will give us peace, and then we will set off for Bronte. In twelve hours we shall be across the water and freed from all the nonsense of his friends, or rather pretended ones. Nothing but an event happening to him could prevent my going, and I am sure you will think so, for unless all matters accord it would bring a hundred of tongues and slanderous reports if I separated from her (which I would do with pleasure the moment we can be united, I want to see her no more) therefore we must manage till we can quit this country or your uncle dies. I love, I never did love anyone else. I never had a dear pledge of love till you gave me one, and you, thank my God, never gave one to anybody else. I think before March is out you will either see us back, or so victorious that we shall insure a glorious issue to our toils. Think what my Emma will feel at seeing return safe, perhaps with a little more fame, her own dear loving Nelson. Never, if I can help it, will I dine out of my ship, or go on shore except duty calls me. Let Sir Hyde have any glory he can catch—I envy him not. You, my beloved Emma, and my country, are the two dearest objects of my fond heart—a heart susceptible and true. Only place confidence in me and you never shall be disappointed. I burn all your dear letters, because it is right for your sake, and I wish you would burn all mine—they can do no good, and will do us both harm if any seizure of them, or the dropping even one of them, would fill the mouth of the world sooner than we intend. My longing for you, both person and conversation, you may readily imagine. What must be my sensations at the idea of sleeping with you, it sets me on fire, even the thought, much more would the reality. I am sure my love and desires are all to you, and if any woman naked were to come to me, even as I am this moment from thinking of you, I hope it might rot off if I would touch her even with my hand. No, my heart, person, and mind is in perfect union of love towards my own dear beloved Emma—the real bosom friend of her, all hers, all Emma's...

My love, my darling angel, my heaven-given wife, the dearest only true wife of her own till death.'

In the same week that Mr Christie, acting on Nelson's instructions, paid £300 for the Romney portrait, Nelson was making an even more determined bid for the 'little more fame' that he had promised Emma would help insure 'a glorious issue for our toils'. On 2 April he fought and won the Battle of Copenhagen, blithely disregarding his commander's instructions to withdraw, and pounding the Danish forts and floating batteries to pieces. Diplomatically it was all very embarrassing, as England had neglected to declare war on Denmark, but nevertheless it quietened England's enemies abroad, and brought Nelson a viscountcy to add to his existing peerage. He returned yet again to Great Yarmouth, to a repeat performance of 'Here the Conquering Hero Comes'. The Admiralty, who were as keen to keep him away from the Hamiltons as he was to be with them, grudgingly granted him three weeks' leave.

There was time for a three-day excursion to Boxhill in Surrey, and a couple of days' quiet fishing from a punt at Staines. Then the Admiralty recalled Nelson to active duty. There was a scare that the French were about to invade and Nelson was placed in supreme command of the coastal defences. He made his headquarters at Deal in Kent, and from here a continuous stream of instructions were sent to Emma. Fanny, who had ceased to figure in his life, still wrote to him but Nelson returned her letters as 'opened but not read'. All he wished for was that as long as Sir William remained alive they remain in England. Once Sir William was dead, then he and Emma would be off to Bronte.

In the meantime he asked Emma to find and buy him a small house close to London, preferably with an acre or two of land. He suggested that she and Sir William used the house on the same basis as they had shared at Palermo. Nothing could have delighted Emma more but Sir William, who readily fell in with the plan, insisted on keeping on the Piccadilly house as well. It was not only pride that made him take this decision; Nelson's offer would have relieved him of a great deal of expense but he was loath to be parted from the round of his cronies in St James's, and in his final years he was determined to enjoy himself.

While Emma went house-hunting, Sir William went to stay with his relations in Warwickshire. In his absence, Emma found a perfect little farmhouse at Merton in Surrey, and having arranged the purchase began to convert and restore it in the manner which she imagined Nelson would like. Sir William greatly approved of her efforts. Late in October he wrote a detailed and chatty bulletin to Nelson, who was tied by his duties to the dubious pleasures of Deal.

'You have nothing but to come and enjoy immediately,' he wrote. 'You have a good mile of pleasant walk around your own farm. It would make you laugh to see Emma and her mother fitting up pig sties and hen coops, and already the canal is enlivened with ducks, and the cock is strutting with his hens about the walks. Your Lordship's plan as to stocking the canal with fish is exactly mine. I will answer for it that in a few months you may command a good dish of fish at a moment's warning.' He continued in a similar vein, remarking that it would be ridiculous for the Admiralty to keep Nelson without leave. Fortunately he was right, and on the last day of the month Nelson drove through the night, with many a change of horses, and took breakfast with Emma and Sir William in the newly decorated morning room at Merton.

X

October 1801–September 1805

The
Merton Ménage

'. . . Le Brun's picture of Emma . . . I
give to my dearest friend Lord
Nelson . . . the most virtuous, loyal
and truly brave character I ever
met with. God bless him
and shame fall on those who do not say
Amen.'

Codicil to the Will of
Sir William Hamilton, March 1803

If Merton was heaven to Nelson and Emma it was far from
being the heaven that history tells us it was. It did not offer
'the mile of pleasant walk around your own farm' that Sir
William had written to Nelson. It was not the comfortable
suburban villa in the Palladian style that Nelson's recent
biographers describe. It had no 'great shrubberies, green
lawns or shady walks', and neither did it have the seventy
acres of farmland with a branch of the River Wandle
flowing gently through them, plenteously stocked with
fish. These were Nelson's dreams, which Sir William was
echoing, and as only one half of their correspondence has
survived, a misleading picture has been created which in its
turn has inspired the canard that Emma foisted on Nelson a
house and an estate which were both too large and too
ostentatious for him, in which she could queen it at his
expense. The truth is that Merton was a slum. True, it was
a slum with possibilities, which Nelson and Emma could

visualise, but slum it was and Nelson was well aware of this before he bought it.

It had been offered to him by the previous owner, a Mr Greaves, who asked £9,000 for the house, furniture and fifty-two acres of land. Emma reported that it had great possibilities, but Nelson's solicitor insisted upon a survey. The survey, which was carried out by a Mr Cockerel, was a damning one.

'The house itself standing on only an acre and a half of ground is surrounded on three sides within twenty yards of it by the property of others, continually in tillage, and is liable to be annoyed by the meanest buildings or other nuisances which may be placed close to it; and within that straightened boundary is circumscribed by a dirty black looking canal, or rather a broad ditch, which keeps the whole place damp.

The house itself consists of an old paltry small dwelling of low stories and very slightly built, at each end of which has been added (very unsubstantially) a very gross room, and nearly the whole of the body has been rendered weak for communication to them. The offices behind are even worse than the house and roof and other parts are so much out of repair that before they can be furnished and comfortably inhabited at least £1,000 must be laid out, exclusive of furniture, and the present furniture of the principal apartments is so inferior that it must also be replaced with new, in which £1,000 more may be easily expended; and when done there will be but one bed chamber in the house fit for a gentleman's accommodation, and that without a dressingroom or other convenience, and not one room to the south of the house.

Add to all this the land is entirely detached by the Turnpike Road and is surrounded by public roads possessing not the least privacy as a place for pleasure—on a dead flat and a clay soil and the whole most scantily worn and out of condition—but if all these things were otherwise, it is wanting in the most essential requisites; there is no kitchen garden or a foot of fruit wall nor any proper situation to make one and no stabling belonging or even a shed or out-houses for cows or other necessary live or dead stock without which the land cannot be occupied—in short it is altogether the worst place under all its circumstances that I ever saw pretending to suit a gentleman's family.'

It was all a far cry from 23 Piccadilly or the Palazzo Sessa, but nevertheless the Hamiltons camped there in the one bedroom 'fit for a gentleman', while Nelson found a cot in one of the others. The three of them stayed there for three days, making detailed plans of the rooms and the grounds, and then returned to London, probably to Sir William's intense relief. Emma's mother came down to supervise the army of painters and plasterers which Nelson mobilised in an effort to make the place habitable for a family Christmas.

A short-lived trial peace with France had just been signed at Amiens and Nelson could look forward to remaining on shore whilst it lasted. It was the beginning of a happy time. Sir William and Emma helped Nelson draw up plans for the remodelling of the house and gardens, and often accompanied him on his almost daily carriage rides to inspect progress and to eat one of Mrs Cadogan's excellent lunches. Sir William bought himself a pony and some books on farming, and took up fishing. Nelson bought a punt and frequently joined him. That autumn turned into an Indian summer, and by Christmas the house was alive to the shouts of children as Nelson's numerous relations descended on them.

These consisted of his brother, the Reverend William Nelson, with his wife, and children Horace and Charlotte, and his two married sisters, Mrs Macham and Mrs Bolton, with their respective husbands and children. Shortly after Christmas his father came for a short stay. The entire Nelson family thoroughly approved of Emma and saw nothing amiss in the strange *ménage à trois*. On the whole Sir William enjoyed himself. He slipped up to London two or three times a week to his beloved auction rooms, and only occasionally complained of the racket and the constantly changing company at Merton. On one occasion he wrote to Greville that, 'It is but reasonable, after having fagged all my life, that my last days should pass off comfortably and quietly. Nothing at present disturbs me but my debt, and the nonsense I am obliged to submit to here to avoid coming to an explosion, which would be attended with many disagreeable effects, and would totally destroy the comfort of the best man and the best friend I have in the world.' This was high praise for Nelson, for Sir William was not so much worried by the fact that Emma and his best friend were lovers but by the charade that he in particular had to play for the benefit of their visitors.

The Treasury had still not paid Sir William, so he was acutely short of money. He and Nelson had agreed to share all expenses, whether at 23 Piccadilly or Merton. This involved keeping two separate staffs as well as the expensive upkeep of the Piccadilly house, which was only used when Sir William took lunch or entertained his friends there. Both houses saw a continuous stream of visitors, ranging from Sir William's diplomatic colleagues to numerous naval officers who, calling formally on Nelson, were usually pressed to stay for a few days. Gradually Sir William began to grudge the money he was paying out on Merton, for though he still worshipped Nelson he had very little time for either his relations or his friends.

To please him, Nelson agreed to accompany him to Oxford where they had both been offered honorary degrees, and then to continue on a tour of the West Country to make an inspection of the Hamilton estates at Milford Haven. Sir William believed that with Nelson's influence his plans for the development of the harbour there could be advanced, and that in consequence the income which he drew from the estate would be considerably increased. The tour was a repeat performance of their visit to Hamilton's cousin, Beckford. They were cheered and fêted in every town, and loaded with the freedoms of numerous cities. Apart from Milford Haven,

Sir William had to take a back seat, for although the expedition was his idea, almost all of Nelson's relations accompanied them. The expenses soared as the standard of conversation dwindled. As soon as it was finished Emma, who was exhausted and ill with jaundice, insisted that she and Sir William take a few days' peace and quiet at Ramsgate. Sir William, who was itching to get back into the swing of things in London, remonstrated with her, and this started the one and only serious row of their marriage. As with anything to do with Sir William it was conducted with style and, curiously enough, in writing. Emma started it by sending him a note.

'As I see it is a pain to you to remain here, let me beg of you to fix your own time for going. Whether I die in Piccadilly or any other spot in England, it's the same to me; but I remember the time when you wished for tranquillity, and now all visiting and bustling is your liking. However I will do what you please, being ever your affectionate and obedient Emma.'

Hamilton promptly dragged Emma back to London, but the lure of fishing soon had him at Merton, until yet again the constant stream of naval friends and relations got on his nerves, for Emma had invited Horace and Charlotte for the school holidays. Nelson himself was busy in the House of Lords.

Sir William became increasingly irritated and when one morning he found that Emma was shopping in London with his carriage, and that Nelson had taken the only other one, his patience gave way. Instead of having it out with her on her return, characteristically he wrote her an ultimatum and pinned it to her dressing table.

'I have passed the last forty years of my life in the hurry and bustle that must necessarily be attendant on a public character. I am arrived at the age when some repose is really necessary, and I promised myself a quiet home, and altho' I was sensible, and said so when I married, that I shou'd be super-annuated when my wife wou'd be in her full beauty and vigour of youth. The time is arrived, and we must make the best of it for the comfort of both parties. Unfortunately our tastes as to the manner of living are very different. I by no means wish to live in solitary retreat, but to have seldom less than twelve or fourteen at table, and those varying continually, is coming back to what was become so irksome to me in Italy during the latter years of my residence in that country. I have no connections out of my own family. I have no complaint to make, but I feel that the whole attention of my wife is given to Ld. N. and his interest at Merton.

I well know the purity of Ld. N's friendship for Emma and me, and I know how very uncomfortable it wou'd make his Lordship, our best friend, if a separation shou'd take place, and am therefore determined to do all in my power to prevent such an extremity, which wou'd be essentially detrimental to all of us. Provided that our expenses in housekeeping do not increase beyond measure (of which I must own I see some danger), I am willing to go on upon our present footing; but as I cannot expect to live many years, every moment to me is precious, and I hope I may be allow'd sometimes to be my own master, and pass my time according to my own inclination, either by going to my fishing parties on the Thames or by going to London to attend the Museum, R. Society, the Tuesday Club and auctions of pictures. I mean to have a light chariot or post chaise by the month, that I may make use of it in London and run backwards and forwards to Merton or Shepperton, etc. This is my plan, and we might go on very well, but I am fully determined not to have more of the very silly altercations that happen but too often between us and embitter the present moments exceedingly. If really one cannot live comfortably together, a wise and well concerted separation is preferable; but I think, considering the probability of my not troubling any party long in this world, the best for us all wou'd be to bear those ills we have rather than flee to those we know not of. I have fairly stated what I have on my mind. There is no time for nonsense or trifling. I know and admire your talents and many excellent qualities, but I am not blind to your defects, and confess having many myself; therefore let us bear and forbear for God's sake.'

Sir William got his carriage. He did not hire one, but bought himself a brand new phaeton and a pair of trotting horses, and hired two extra grooms to tend them. Emma and Nelson had recognised the danger signals. Emma became more amenable, and Nelson, selling some of his presentation gold boxes, paid half their cost. Sir William was in his element again, frequently staying overnight in London and dropping friendly notes to Emma describing his evenings. 'The Duke of Queensberry chose to dine alone. Lord Warwick is gone to the Castle, so I dined alone at home on pickled salmon, pigeon and peas, cold lamb and Tart—Good port which after every delicacy is most necessary...' Possibly it was the latter which he had most missed at Merton.

Emma was furiously busy, but oblivious to all criticism except Sir William's. She adored helping with Nelson's nieces and nephews, and enjoyed the somewhat vulgar company of her lover's friends. The events of one weekend at Merton are given in a fascinating pair of letters which neither author knew the other was writing. A party of Nelson's and Sir William's friends had been invited for the weekend, the guest of honour being Lord Minto, an old diplomatic colleague of Sir William. The Hamiltons and Nelson were trying to persuade him to recommend Nelson's clerical brother for a deanery or other promotion within the Church; Nelson had already tried to do so through official channels and had been roundly snubbed for his pains. The trouble was that the Rev. Dr William Nelson was an uncouth and boring man, intensely mean, and never with a good word to say about anyone. He revelled in being heir to Nelson's title. He had jumped at an honorary degree of Doctor of Letters which Nelson had obtained for him from Oxford but was content to let Emma look after his daughter Charlotte and for her to have his son Horace for the holidays from Eton, the latter a luxury Nelson was paying for. He was not content with being the plain Rev. Dr William Nelson and wanted promotion. Emma tried her best and wrote to his wife reporting on the weekend.

'Lord Minto arrived at dinner time and we passed a most pleasant evening. After supper I began on purpose to tell him of all the ill-usage (before Nelson) that he had suffered of the doctor's not being provided for. He was astonished and outraged, and when Nelson said "I only wanted a canonship or a deanery for my only brother" Lord Minto answered, "Fye Fye, he ought not to accept that. The minister ought to have thrown a bishoprick at you, saying, 'Give it to your brother, you are our saviour'." He then said that he wished only to be minister to do it. So you see my dear friend this will be of use... He dotes and worships Nelson, he is a great friend of ours.

...We shall be nineteen at dinner. Lord Minto is charmed with Charlotte. He says she will be a beautiful woman and he likes her manner ... Miss Furze [a school friend of Charlotte Nelson, also staying] ate so much in the evening that she vomited before us all. Lord Minto played [the piano]. Mrs Tyson was drunk and when she talked nonsense her husband tipped her the wink and she held her tongue ... I am writing and they (the men) are talking politics.'

Lord Minto, who had obviously done some flattering himself that evening, also wrote an account of the same weekend.

'I went to Lord Nelson on Saturday to dinner and returned today in the forenoon. The whole establishment and way of life is such as to make me angry ... Sir William will not be long in her way, and she probably indulges a hope that she may survive Lady Nelson. In the meantime she and Sir William and the whole set of them are living with him at his expense. She is in high looks ... she goes on cramming Nelson with trowelfulls of flattery which he goes on taking as quietly as a child does pap. The love she makes him is not only ridiculous, but disgusting; not only the rooms, but the whole house, staircase and all are covered with nothing but pictures of her and him, of all sizes and sorts, and representations of his naval actions, coats-of-arms, pieces of plate in his honour ... etc—an excess of vanity ... If it was Lady Hamilton's house there might be a pretence for it; to make his own a mere looking glass to view himself all day is bad taste.'

Lord Minto was unkind to Sir William when he said he was living with Nelson at Nelson's expense. He was making an effort to share the bills, but though he and Nelson kept a careful account, Sir William was well behind in settling his share, for he was still waiting for his money from the Treasury. He did have some £7,000 in Treasury bonds, but he needed the income they provided for his daily expenses at 23 Piccadilly. He was living on borrowed money, and now on borrowed time. At the end of March 1803, that time ran out. He was taken seriously ill with bronchitis, and Nelson and Emma carried him up to Piccadilly where they and Emma's mother took turns to sit beside him for six days and nights. One evening Charles Greville called, and finding Mrs Cadogan at the bedside, asked her to leave the room. Sir William, who had not spoken for some time, apparently did so at length to Greville; or at least Greville claimed that he did, in an affidavit he presented when applying for probate of the Will. Greville swore on oath that Sir William said it was his wish that Greville have his £7,000 and that he did not wish the services of a priest.

Sir William died four days later in Emma's arms, with Nelson holding his hand. In his Will he left Emma £800 a year, and charged Greville to pay her debts. Greville never did, claiming that Sir William meant them to be settled when his claim against the Treasury was paid. Nelson was left a pair of sporting guns and, in Sir William's words, 'The copy of Madame Le Brun's picture of Emma in enamel by Bone I give to my dearest friend Lord Nelson, Duke of Bronte, a very small token of the great regard I have for his Lordship, the most virtuous, loyal and truly brave character I ever met with. God Bless him and shame fall on those who do not say Amen.'

It was a wry codicil, probably designed to stifle gossip against his friend. In that way it was generous, but in another it was ironic, for Sir William was well aware that his lordship already possessed not only the picture but its subject.

Greville acted strangely to Emma. As long as it did not cost him a penny, he assisted her. He helped her prepare a petition to the government complaining that she had no widow's pension, when even the widow of a consul received at least £600 a year. Nelson, too, helped her in this, but despite a great deal of effort and the re-commendations of Pitt, Addington, and Lord Minto, no pension ever materialised.

Where money and property were concerned, Greville was his usual mean self. He gave Emma a month to quit 23 Piccadilly, and stipulated that the contents that Sir William had left her related only to what was in the house at the time he wrote the Will, which was before they had moved in. Eventually Emma managed to salvage some linen and a few items of furniture. She complained to Nelson, but there was little he could do. For propriety's sake he had moved out of the house the day Sir William died, and was sharing an apartment with Greville. His accounts show that two weeks with Greville cost him £67, or in present-day terms about £2000 a week. Greville was far too clever for the Admiral to argue with. Thereafter Greville saw little of Emma, and although he paid her allowance regularly, he deducted every expense that he could think of, including Sir Wiliam's arrears of income tax and debts that he had left to local tradesmen, wine merchants, etc., on the grounds that Emma had, and was continuing to enjoy, whatever it was Sir William had purchased.

At a time when Emma needed a man's advice and help more than at any time in her life, Nelson had to leave her. War with France broke out again on 18 May 1803 and the same day Nelson hoisted his flag in HMS *Victory* at

Portsmouth. Before he left, on what was to be an absence
of two years, he and Emma went through their finances.
He had an income of £5,500 a year, and Emma around £400
when Greville got around to paying it. Not counting Sir
William's debts, Emma had debts of some £700 of her own
which Greville refused to settle until the Treasury met Sir
William's claims. Of Nelson's money, the allowance to his
wife and tax took over half, which left him a balance of
around £2,600 a year. He kept £1,400 for himself and made
Emma an allowance of £1,200 a year payable at £100 a
month with which to keep Horatia, run Merton and his
farm, and pay interest on the mortgages he had incurred
when he bought the property and on a further £4,000 he
had borrowed to buy some surrounding land. In addition
there were Horace's fees at Eton, and three pensioners to
whom he allowed £100 a year apiece. It was obvious to
them both that they would have to be very careful. Emma
had less than the income Fanny Nelson received in
alimony, and on which she found difficulty in living in
genteel retirement in Bath. And Emma had all the
responsibilities.

Nevertheless, the two of them decided to go ahead with
their plans for Merton. There were rooms to be built, the
farm developed, crops to be sown and bills to be paid.
Improvident as it may seem, jointly they proceeded with
their ideas, counting on Emma at last getting a pension
from the government; on Greville being as generous as Sir
William had meant him to be; and, of course, both of them
confident that in a matter of weeks, Nelson would repeat
his triumph over the French and return home, rich with
honours and prize money. It was a childish decision, but
then both of them were children at heart. There was also
one pressing reason for alterations at Merton. A nursery
was needed, for Emma was pregnant again. On 13 May
1803, shortly before he sailed, he and Emma attended to
one important detail. Horatia was christened at
Marylebone Church as Horatia Nelson Thompson. Her
birth date was falsified as having been on 29 October 1800,
to give credence to the plan her parents had in mind, which

was to pretend that she had been born before either of them returned to England from Naples, and that they had adopted her. With this last detail attended to, Nelson sailed after the French.

While Nelson was away, his relations used Merton as a family home. Emma spent most of her time there, but propriety dictated that she keep a separate establishment of her own. She rented a small house in Clarges Street off Piccadilly, and set to work carrying out Nelson's instructions at Merton. In almost every letter of his there were instructions about the house or garden: a path to be re-routed, gates to be built, netting to be placed around the water's edge so that Horatia, who was now living there, would not fall in. The instructions were legion, and all were carried out to the letter. In the meantime she continued to look after Horace and Charlotte, and to feed and house his naval friends. Early in 1804 Nelson's second child was born after a difficult pregnancy. It was a girl, christened Emma, but it caught smallpox and died in the same spring, to be buried in Paddington Churchyard. Emma consoled herself by taking all the children to Ramsgate for some sea-bathing.

Nelson's letters were her major consolation, as were hers to him. At times she missed him so terribly that she begged him to strike his flag and retire. She tried to keep her money worries from him, but the bills kept mounting up. Eventually she found that she could pledge her own income from Sir William's estate in order to obtain credit; in this way she pledged most of it to money-lenders in order to pay for the improvements at Merton, thereby creating the setting she knew her lover wanted. In this she was helped by a windfall, as Nelson was suddenly paid the prize money he had sued Earl St Vincent for. It has been alleged that Emma blued this in one burst of extravagance. The opposite is true. Instead of using it to pay the bills, she settled the outstanding mortgage on the extra land Nelson had bought.

Sometimes she went to stay with Nelson's married sisters. There was a week in Norfolk with Mrs Bolton, a week at Southend with Mrs Matcham, and a rather colourless month at Canterbury where the Rev. Dr William Nelson had at last acquired a modest deanery. However all the time she was away, the bills followed her. Canterbury was spoilt by an urgent letter from her mother asking for £13 to pay the haymakers, while the butcher's and baker's bills for that month, July 1805, came to over £100. As she was away the whole month, it shows how Nelson's total allowance of £100 a month was grossly insufficient, for Merton had many mouths to feed. There was Nelson's butler, valet, secretary, three kitchen maids beside the cook, two parlour maids, two gardeners, a cowman, two grooms, and the open house Nelson insisted on keeping. There was a nursery maid, singing teachers for Charlotte, a tutor for Horace, Emma's mother; the list was endless. To complicate matters still further, many of Sir William's old friends liked to call. The Dukes of Queensbury, Sussex and Clarence looked in on their way to Brighton, and who knows what expense these uninvited guests put the household to. When Nelson at last returned from his two-year abortive chase after the French, Emma was almost £8,000 in debt. She had survived by paying interest on the debt from her pension, and because her creditors knew that it was Lord Nelson who was the real debtor and there was little to be gained by dunning him.

Nelson arrived at Merton on 20 August 1805. It was the first and only time in their relationship that the two of them were alone without Sir William. It was to be a fleeting visit, for he was to sail as soon as it was confirmed that the French were in Cadiz, and his ships had been refitted. It was a wonderful three weeks, though each knew they had very little time. Most days there were family parties, and in the evenings Nelson dined with his friends and relations. The butcher's bill for that belated honeymoon was almost £400. The visitors to Merton were legion, even Lord Minto coming again and charitably noting that 'Lord Nelson was remarkably well, full of spirits. His conversation is a cordial in these low times. Lady Hamilton has improved and added to the house and place extremely well ... she is a clever being after all ... the passion is as hot as ever.'

Merton had now become a tranquil and beautiful home. Now the lawns and shrubberies, the walks and the pretty little farm with its model dairy were a reality. Nelson was delighted. He christened the little river the Nile, and the balcony outside the drawing room his quarterdeck. He played with Horatia in every spare moment and dreaded the summons that he knew was coming. It arrived at dawn on 2 September. The Admiralty sent a messenger to say that the French were at Cadiz and offered him supreme command. It was more of an order than an invitation, but nevertheless for a while he seriously thought of turning it down. Then he accepted, and arranged to arrive at Portsmouth at dawn on 13 September.

On the night of 12 September, Emma and Nelson took communion together. Shortly afterwards his carriage arrived, and they began to say goodbye for what both of them knew in their hearts was probably the last time. Nelson suddenly slipped upstairs and spent some ten minutes in prayer beside the sleeping Horatia. Then he ran out to his carriage. At the last moment indecision took him. Four times he got into the carriage and four times he came out again for just one more goodbye. After the last embrace on the 'quarterdeck' he came down the steps. Emma must have stiffened his resolve, for he said to his nephew, George Matcham, who was holding the horses, 'Brave Emma. If there were more Emmas, there could be more Nelsons.' As his carriage rattled down the drive, he pulled out his pocket book and wrote the following prayer.

'Friday night this half past ten drove from dear, dear Merton, where I left all that I hold dear in this world to go and serve my King and Country. May the Great God whom I adore enable me to fulfil the expectations of my country and if it is his good pleasure that I should return, my thanks will never cease to be offered up to the throne of his mercy. If it is his good providence to cut short my days upon earth, I bow with the greatest submission, relying that he will protect those dear to me, that I leave behind. His will be done, Amen, Amen, Amen.'

Everyone noticed the change in Nelson when he took command. He was gentler, less vain, going out of his way to be kind and courteous to colleagues; more than ever he was desperately in love. Above all, his letters and despatches show that he firmly believed that he was going to his death, and possibly his new attitude was one of expiation and perhaps also an effort to ask of the God to whom he wrote another respite. Before he left Portsmouth he remarked to his stores officer, 'I shall outdo my former achievements, but I shall not return to enjoy the glories I acquire.' Shortly after the masts of the French fleet were sighted, Nelson called a conference aboard the *Victory*. As the captains prepared to return to their own ships, Nelson took Captain Blackwood, a frequent guest at Merton, aside. 'Goodbye my dear Blackwood,' he said, 'we shall not meet again.'

XI

October 1805

Trafalgar

'Doctor, I have not been a great
sinner . . . remember that I leave
Lady Hamilton and my daughter
Horatia as a legacy to my country
. . . Thank God I have done my
duty.'

Last words of Lord Nelson,
Trafalgar, 21 October 1805

When Nelson left Portsmouth on 15 September, 'with three sail of the line' as the official communiqué reported the departure, he knew as well as the Admiralty Lords in Whitehall that England's destiny sailed with him. He had sent ahead a fast frigate bearing his personal orders to Collingwood's fleet 'that in these dire circumstances the usual naval honours due to an admiral arriving to take up his command must be waived in the interest of secrecy . . .' No colours were hoisted and no guns fired when the *Victory* reached her destination off Cadiz on 29 September, Nelson's forty-seventh birthday. It was too important a battle to run the risk of alerting the eighteen French and fifteen Spanish ships to the arrival of English reinforcements led by the greatest naval commander in her history. A few years earlier Nelson would have been elated by the prospect of a major battle with a vast fleet which for once was in no position to evade him. But now both sides were overcome with their sense of the impending battle. A distinct note of awe and humility characterizes the despatches of the French and Spanish admirals, just as it does Nelson's own notes, reports, memoranda and prayers. His apprehension, first felt in Horatia's nursery at Merton, had never left him.

The more one examines Nelson's statements and thoughts at this time, the clearer their leitmotif of morbidity becomes. It had always been present in his character; perhaps the most glaring example was his macabre idea of inspecting his own coffin, which had been constructed for him from the mainmast of the *Orient* after she had exploded so spectacularly at the Battle of the Nile. It may be that Nelson understood, on some intuitive level, that the kind of glory which he craved could only be accorded—such was the nature of the English people—to a national hero who had made the ultimate sacrifice. Only blood could liberate his dull countrymen's capacity for deification—and also, incidentally, persuade them that it was appropriate to give some monetary expression to their collective gratitude.

On the voyage out from Portsmouth Nelson had decided to adopt a plan devised twenty years earlier by a Captain John Clerk, in a little known book on naval tactics. Clerk had considered the problem of a fleet having to engage a numerically superior enemy who was possibly reluctant to come to battle. He had advised an attack in two or three columns sailing in line ahead and approaching the enemy at right angles. The enemy line of battle would then be cut into sections, and Clerk's device was to isolate the forward or downwind section so that it would have to waste time and tack up into the wind to rejoin the battle. In this way the attacking fleet would reduce the odds against it by the size of the enemy section left downwind, and conceal until the last moment the fact that it was not going to turn from its angle of attack and take up the conventional naval position of two parallel lines of ships hurling broadsides at each other. Clerk's final recommendation was that having fragmented the enemy battle line, the fight could be resolved by close-quarter fighting.

History has christened this technique 'The Nelson

Touch', but this phrase was never used by Nelson to his officers. It appeared in his letter to Emma written after he had briefed his officers. Nelson remarked that his officers were elated at the idea of climbing aboard an enemy, and his use of the words 'The Nelson Touch' were a private and wholly personal joke shared between them, probably invented by Emma. When his letters were published some years later—without Emma's consent—historians avidly seized the phrase and put it into a context for which it was never intended. The scheme Nelson explained to them verbally was embodied in the so-called 'Nelson Memorandum' which has often been cited for its inspired mixture of tradition and innovation as the apogee of naval genius. The fact remains that Nelson's basic strategy—to disguise the point of attack—was as convincing on the day as twenty years earlier Clerk had made it look on paper.

Captain Blackwood, who went on board *Victory* on the eve of the battle, recorded that Nelson displayed none of the excitement that had been so apparent before the great encounters of Copenhagen and Aboukir Bay. Nelson asked Blackwood, thus ensuring him of a place in the history books, whether he thought it appropriate to issue a signal as an 'Order of the Day'. Blackwood replied that the enthusiasm of the fleet was so manifest it was unnecessary. The 'Nelson Memorandum', as he pointed out, had the advantage of simplicity in one essential—the question of proximity. As Nelson had written: 'In case signals can neither be seen or perfectly understood, no Captain can do very wrong if he places his ship alongside that of an Enemy...' To later generations, more cynical about war, and more concerned about casualties, such instructions (not unlike those issued to the Japanese Kamikaze pilots before the Battle of Midway) might seem the reverse of inspirational. Yet their impact on captains hungry for prize money, and aware that in proximity resided a certain safety, cannot be doubted.

Nelson understood that the question of morale would very likely be conclusive. Accordingly, despite his own restrained mood, he strove to be as theatrical as possible.

Ignoring Blackwood's reply about the signal, his flags spelled out the message which has become a fixture in the history books. In the same spirit he paraded in his admiral's frockcoat, its already splendid gold embellishments further heightened by the four stars he wore on the left breast. With an eye on history, and his thoughts no doubt once more on the English public and the future of Emma and the baby, he also dictated a message which for moral uplift could not have been improved on by any Victorian:

'Now I can do no more. We must trust to the Great Disposer of all events, and the justice of our cause. I thank God for this great opportunity of doing my duty.'

The seamen, in less elevated vein, repeated the traditional Royal Navy blasphemy reserved for those occasions when an incoming broadside was imminent: 'For what we are about to receive may the Lord make us truly thankful.'

Victory's surgeon, Mr Beatty, was thinking in similar terms, but worried about Nelson in his ostentatious best uniform which made him a natural magnet for the sharp-shooters, the French and Spanish always positioned to snipe at officers from the mizzen tops. Beatty communicated his fears to Dr Scott, the chaplain, and also to the official secretary and historian, who confusingly was also called Scott.

On the quarterdeck of the *Victory* Captain Blackwood, in what seemed to him, privately, an over-optimistic assessment designed to keep Nelson's morale high, forecast that they would capture fourteen of the French leviathans which were firing their first tentative broadsides. It was his last word, as he had been ordered to follow Prowse with the same instructions for ships of the line and rejoin his own frigate. Nelson's reaction was more optimistic, but it was fatalistic. He repeated his earlier remark: 'God bless you, Blackwood. We shall have 20 prizes but I shall never see you again.'

Blackwood, no introvert, never apparently allowed himself to consider that this message might contain any ambiguity about his own prospects. It was the safety of

Nelson, provocative to the point of recklessness on *Victory*'s poop, which exercised Blackwood's mind as Nelson, steering two points further to the north than *Royal Sovereign* in order to bisect the enemy's line of escape into Cadiz, now for the first time came within musket range of an old enemy, the *Santissima Trinidad*, an enormous four-decker towering above the tiny but infinitely manoeuvrable *Victory*. He had cause to worry: Scott, the admiral's secretary, was killed by a cannon shot while talking to Hardy only thirty feet from Nelson himself. At noon *Victory* had been under fire for almost an hour. Her right-angled approach had prevented her from bringing her own broadsides into action; now the moment of truth had come. Nelson had said to Hardy: 'This is too warm work to last long.' It now became clear there was no chance of breaking the enemy line without ramming one of their ships. *Victory* crashed into the French three-decker *Redoutable*, who received her with a broadside which passed through her tops, and an enfilade of musketry from her own snipers aloft which accounted for twenty-three marines killed or wounded. The situation would have been fatal for *Victory* but Captain Harvey, commanding the *Temeraire*, now fell on board the *Redoutable* from the other side.

It was a ball from the mizzen top of *Redoutable* which struck Nelson on the left shoulder, entering via the epaulette. He apparently had no doubt about the outcome of the wound, telling Hardy that he had been shot through the breast-bone. His face was covered with a handkerchief and two sailors carried him down to the dark cockpit where Surgeon Beatty was at work among the dead and dying. It took half an hour to move the wounded admiral through the chaos and lay his body on a midshipman's pallet.

No surgery was possible, or even attempted. Instead Hardy fanned him with a chart, while a relay of seamen brought lemonade for over four hours into the afternoon to try and alleviate the thirst which gripped him. When Hardy returned to the poop, Nelson, convinced in his delirium that his old comrade must have been killed, screamed out for him again and again. When Hardy returned, he reported that the musketeer who had shot Nelson had himself been accounted for thanks to two midshipmen called Pollard and Collingwood (a distant relation of the Vice-Admiral). Neither this information, nor the inaccurate news that fifteen prizes had been taken, was much consolation for the dying man. His main thoughts were for Emma, bequeathing her his hair as well as his papers. When the surgeon inquired about the pain, he said it was so great that he wished he were dead, and then added with commendable candour, but in a voice so low that it was hard to hear: 'Yet I would like to live a little longer.'

There has been much disagreement as to what precisely Nelson said and to whom on his deathbed. Suffice it to say he worried equally about Emma, his child and the safety of his fleet, stressing the need to anchor immediately after the battle as a storm was brewing. Perhaps he had a premonition of the storms that lay ahead of Emma.

XII

October 1805–January 1815

Lady Hamilton Expects

'Disappointed still, was still deceiv'd.'
William Cowper

Emma had not been well. Whenever she was nervous she suffered from a form of psoriasis, and on 6 November she stayed late in bed. Nelson's sister, Mrs Bolton, was sitting beside the bed, and they were planning what to do to amuse the children. Suddenly Mrs Bolton looked up and said, 'Listen.' The two women strained their ears. 'I think,' said Emma, 'that I hear the Tower guns, some victory, perhaps in Germany?' 'Perhaps,' replied Mrs Bolton, 'it may be news from my brother.' 'Impossible, surely, there is not time.' As the two of them spoke, they heard a carriage coming up the drive, and five minutes later a maid announced that a Mr Whitby from the Admiralty was waiting below. Emma told her to show him up.

Mr Whitby entered the room, and in a low voice said, 'We have gained a great victory.' 'Never mind your victory,' replied Emma, 'where are my letters?' Whitby was unable to speak and began to cry silently. Emma screamed and fainted. When she came round she was unable to speak or even cry. She sat silent and withdrawn for almost ten hours. Nelson's sisters tried to comfort her, and two days later his brother the Rev. Dr arrived at Merton with the Will. It was opened in Emma's bedroom, with the family sitting round. That same morning it had been announced that the grasping little clergyman had been created an Earl in honour of his brother, and had been granted a pension of £5,000 a year for life; and that in due course Parliament would vote him sufficient money to purchase an estate appropriate to his new station.

The Will contained few surprises. Emma was left Merton and its contents, a cash sum of £2,000, and £500 a year for life secured on the income from the Bronte estate. Horatia was left £4,000 in trust for her until she was eighteen, with the income until then going to Emma for Horatia's education. In each case, the new Earl Nelson was appointed the trustee for the regular payment of these bequests. At this time all those present were unaware that Nelson might well have written a codicil to his Will while waiting to do battle with the French.

There was a codicil and it arrived with Captain Hardy when the *Victory* limped home on 4 December, carrying Nelson's body, preserved in a cask of brandy, and his last letters to Emma and Horatia. Before any of these documents are examined, it is important to put Emma's position in its proper context. She was the mistress of a dead naval hero who had a wife who was still alive. She had not been accepted at Court, and had an unpleasant but not wholly deserved reputation. So far she had not offended against the code of the time by openly embarrassing anybody, and in government circles there were those who felt strongly that she deserved a pension, either as the widow of a distinguished and faithful Ambassador, or even as the mistress of Nelson. She had also carried out excellent work for the British cause whilst she had been in Naples and Palermo. Her supporters included the Prime Minister, her ducal friends, even the Prince of Wales, who had made his peace with Nelson. Many of Nelson's naval friends supported her claim for a pension, and if Emma had played her cards correctly she would probably have obtained one. However her hopes were not to be realised. On 22 November, extracts from certain of Nelson's letters were published which showed only too openly what their relationship had been. How the letters reached the papers is still a mystery. There is a store of circumstantial evidence that the new Earl had borrowed them, taken copies, and then handed the copies to the editor of the paper who lived close to Merton Court and with whom the Earl had dined after reading the Will. The letters gravely embarrassed many of Emma's supporters. She had offended against '*bienséance*' and from henceforth was out in the cold. Nelson was still unburied and here was his mistress selling his confidences to the gutter press for a handful of silver. It was a vicious libel on Emma, and in the cold light of history, remarkably convenient to the new Earl. The outcry over the publication of the letters was still raging when Captain Hardy arrived with the codicil. It was written as follows:

'October the Twenty-first, one thousand eight hundred and five, then in sight of the Combined Fleets of France and Spain, distant about Ten Miles. Whereas the Eminent Services of Emma Hamilton, Widow of the Right Honourable Sir William Hamilton, have been of the very greatest service to our King and Country, to my knowledge, without her receiving any reward from either our King or country, first, that she obtained the King of Spain's letter in 1796 to his brother, the King of Naples acquainting him of his intention to declare War against England; from which Letter the Ministry sent out orders to then Sir John Jervis, to strike a stroke, if opportunity offered, against either the Arsenals of Spain, or her Fleets. That neither of these was done is not the fault of Lady Hamilton, the opportunity might have been offered. Secondly the British Fleet under my command, could never have returned the second time to Egypt, had not Lady Hamilton's influence with the Queen of Naples caused letters to be wrote to the Governor of Syracuse, that he was to encourage the Fleet being supplied with everything, should they put into any Port in Sicily. We put into Syracuse, and received every supply, went to Egypt, and destroyed the French Fleet.

Could I have rewarded these services I would not now call upon my Country; but as that has not been in my power, I leave Emma Lady Hamilton, therefore, a Legacy to my King and Country, that they will give her an ample provision to maintain her Rank in Life. I also leave to the beneficence of my Country my adopted daughter, Horatia Nelson Thompson; and I desire she will use in future the name of Nelson only.

These are the only favours I ask of my King and Country at this moment when I am going to fight their Battle. May God bless my King and Country, and all those who I hold dear. My Relations, it is needless to mention: they will of course be amply provided for.

Nelson and Bronte'

Witness: Henry Blackwood
         T. M. Hardy

The Earl felt that as Emma had been left to the nation, he personally was absolved of all responsibility. He went even further and announced that he was unable to pay Emma the £500 a year Nelson had left her, as the estate could not afford it. This was a palpable lie and eventually, a few weeks before Emma died, he paid one instalment, nine years in arrears. The nation did nothing about the codicil either. 'Perhaps,' said the wiseacres in Whitehall, 'when all the fuss has died down, we might manage a discreet something, if in the meantime you keep quiet and don't embarrass any of us.' Emma's consolation were Nelson's last letters to Horatia and herself. That to Horatia was simple.

'My dearest Angel, I was made happy by the pleasure of receiving your letter of 19 September, and I rejoice to hear that you are so very good a girl, and love my dear Lady Hamilton, who most dearly loves you. Give her a kiss for me. The combined fleets of the enemy are now reported to be coming out of Cadiz; and therefore I answer your letter, my dearest Horatia, to mark to you that you are ever uppermost in my thoughts. I shall be sure of your prayers for my safety, conquest and speedy return to dear Merton, and our dearest good Lady Hamilton. Be a good girl, mind what Miss Connor says to you. Receive, my dearest

Horatia, the affectionate parental blessing of your Father.

Nelson and Bronte'

His letter to Emma was unfinished:

'My dearest beloved Emma, the dear friend of my bosom, the signal has been made that the enemy's combined fleet are coming out of port. We have very little wind, so that I have no hopes of seeing them before tomorrow. May the God of Battles crown my endeavours with success; at all events, I will take care that my name shall ever be most dear to you and Horatia, both of whom I love as much as my own life. And as my last writing before the battle will be to you, so I hope in God that I shall live to finish my letter after the battle. May Heaven bless you prays your—

Nelson and Bronte'

Next day he added:

'20 October. In the morning, we were close to the mouth of the Straits, but the wind had not come far enough to the westward to allow the combined fleets to weather the shoals off Trafalgar; but they were counted as far as forty sail of ships-of-war, which I suppose to be thirty-four of the line, and six frigates. A group of them was seen off the lighthouse of Cadiz this morning, but it blows so very fresh and thick weather, that I rather believe they will go into the harbour before night. May God Almighty give us success over these fellows, and enable us to get a peace...'

All Emma had was the expectation of £2,000 when Nelson's Will was proved, together with Merton and its contents. Coupled to the latter were her and Nelson's debts of some £8,000 which she was servicing from the income from Sir William's estate. She had next to nothing to live on, but at least she could educate Horatia. Now was a time for decision, and unfortunately, if perhaps characteristically, she made the wrong one.

It would have been the common-sense course to have sold Merton and paid her debts, and then she would still have had enough left over to purchase a smaller house where she and her mother could bring up Horatia. With her debts paid, her income would have been increased and she would have had more than enough to live quite comfortably. Emma took the opposite course. Merton was all that she had left to remind her of Nelson. Although the new Earl was behaving abominably, she was still looking after his children, Mrs Bolton and her children were living with her almost permanently, and there was still the staff. These had been Nelson's servants and what was to become of them? Mrs Bolton's husband was increasingly short of money, and there were the pensions to pay to old Mrs Graffer whose husband had laid out the English Garden in Naples so long ago. There was the payment of 'Old Blindy', the blind mistress of Nelson's brother Maurice, who had died there previously, and numerous small stipends to some of the poorer members of her mother's family who had been dependent on her for many years.

Emma was convinced that eventually the government would reward her handsomely and she was equally sure that they would take care of Nelson's sisters. Until they did, she and they had to have money to live on. Mrs Bolton, Mrs Matcham and herself held a council of war. As a result Emma's mother wrote asking the indulgence of the government to provide for Nelson's sisters. In the meantime, until the government made their decision known, Emma pledged Merton to a rich banker neighbour, a man called Abraham Goldsmid. He lent £2,000 apiece to each of them, and Emma was responsible for the interest. Six months later the government granted the Earl £90,000, and each of the sisters £15,000. They paid back their share to Mr Goldsmid, but Emma, who had got nothing, went on paying interest.

Emma spent her £2,000 living as she had always done. She still kept open house to any professed friend or acquaintance of Nelson, and many were the sharks who took her hospitality and gave nothing in return. Any old sailor calling at the door was sure of a guinea or two, and there was no shortage of those once the fleet had been paid off.

She was reckless, she was absurdly generous, and with hindsight she was remarkably stupid. Eventually the Earl delivered the *coup de grâce*. He descended on Merton and claimed all of Nelson's trophies, silver plate, swords and decorations; in fact, all the trappings of the hero with which to bedeck his new station in life. Their loss sickened Emma, who could not believe anyone could be so petty. At the same time he collected his children and informed Emma that she would have to pay any outstanding bills that Nelson had left which related to Merton. On totting them up, it was obvious even to Emma that she was bankrupt.

Emma still had friends. There was her neighbour, Mr Goldsmid. There was Sir John Perring, a former Lord Mayor of London, Alexander Davison, who had been Nelson's man of business, and a clutch of neighbours from Merton. On 25 November 1808 they gathered in Sir John's house at Broad Street in the City of London to formulate a scheme to rescue Emma from her creditors and herself. They have left a precise account of their meeting and their plan. In reading it, it is important to understand that the word annuities covered both money-lenders and those pensioners of Nelson's whom she was still supporting.

'At a meeting of the friends of Lady Hamilton, held at the house of Sir John Perring, Bart., 25 November 1808.

Present

Sir John Perring	Mr McClure	Mr Nichol
Mr Davison	Mr Goldsmid	Mr Wilson
Mr Moore	Sir Robert Barclay	Mr Lavie
Mr Gooch		

Mr Dawson attending as Solicitor to Lady Hamilton.
Read   A letter from Lady Hamilton addressed to the gentlemen attending the meeting.
Read   A list of debts delivered in by Mr Davison as obtained by advertisement, also a list of additional debts delivered in by Lady Hamilton herself, the whole debt

estimated at £8,000 exclusive of £10,000 required to pay off annuities.

Upon consideration of the property possessed by Lady Hamilton the same was ascertained as follows:

Books	£1,500
Wine	2,000
Statues, Vases, China, Pictures, and other articles of fancy	1,500
Furniture and Fixtures	1,500
House & 32 Acres	7,500
40 Acres	3,500
Taken at a very low rate	£17,500

The above property being independent of her annuities under the Wills of Sir William Hamilton and Lord Nelson, and her claim on government.

RESOLVED   That an assignment of the whole of Lady Hamilton's property be taken, and that the same be made to:

Sir John Perring, Bart.   Richard Wilson, Esq.
Alexander Davison, Esq.   and
Abraham Goldsmid, Esq.   Germain Lavie, Esq.

as Trustees for Sale, etc.

That in order to afford an immediate relief the following sums be advanced by

Alexr. Davison	One thousand pounds
Abm. Goldsmid	One thousand pounds
John Gooch	Five hundred pounds
Richd. Wilson	Five hundred pounds
Sir Robert Barclay	Five hundred pounds
John Perring	Two hundred pounds

to be secured by the said Trust with interest.

That the money collected by the above advances be applied in payment of all incumbrances absolutely necessary to be immediately discharged. That all the creditors be supplied to execute the Debt of Trust, and to agree to accept payment out of the Trust Estate.

That pending the Trust Lady Hamilton be allowed to receive her annuities, but in case of deficiency the same shall be applied in liquidating the balance.

That the Trustees be a Committee to follow up the claim on government, in which all the friends of Lady Hamilton be requested to co-operate. That the Trustees do go to market in the most advantageous mode possible, so as not to injure the property by a premature sale.

Signed	Robert Barclay	John Gooch
	Alexr. Davison	A. McClure
	F. Moore	George Nicol
	Abm. Goldsmid	Richd. Wilson
	Germain Lavie	John Perring

Emma paid off the servants and left Merton for the last time. By now her immediate family had grown to include Horatia, her mother, her mother's sister Mrs Connor, and five of her six Connor nieces. Emma was their sole support. In addition there was an old lady called Dame Francis, who had been in charge of the nursery at Merton and had nowhere else to go, and a literary hack called James Harrison who had moved in at Merton with the specious scheme of writing a biography of Nelson. The agreement was that Emma was to supply him with bed and board in exchange for half of the royalties. Needless to say, she never got them.

On 23 April the following spring Charles Greville died, unlamented by one and all, though at least whatever proportion of her allowance under Sir William's Will that he had calculated was due to her had been paid promptly. His heir and Emma's new trustee was Sir Robert Fulke Greville, who had no head for business whatsoever, and whose monthly cheques were frequently either in arrears or not made out properly. However a degree of help came from an unexpected quarter. The old Duke of Queensberry lent her a house at Richmond until she could find lodgings, and secretly guaranteed her overdraft at Coutts' bank—for a modest amount.

Emma found lodgings at Dover Street for the majority of her swollen household, and settling in, promptly fell ill with another attack of jaundice. This turned into dropsy, and her figure began to swell as fluid began to settle in her legs and abdomen. The medical treatment of frequent bleeding and a daily intake of several pints of fluid—preferably porter or weak beer—complicated her condition and set up a chain of urinary and liver troubles; probably hepatitis, though Emma called it jaundice. The main side-effect apart from a greatly increased figure was a constant feeling of being overtired. It was a miserable year. There was hardly any money, and one by one her last treasures went to the pawn shops. From her bed she wrote to everyone she could think of: to the Treasury, begging for a pension; to Earl Nelson, begging him to pay her the £500 a year which Nelson had left her, and of which she had not received a penny; a letter to Sir Harry Featherstonehaugh, which must have cost her her last morsel of pride, and which brought gifts of game and tepid invitations to visit Uppark 'when times were quieter'. Nelson's brother-in-law Mr Matcham sent her £100 and on Christmas Eve the artist Baxter, who had lived near Merton and whom Emma had encouraged to come and draw in the garden, brought her a goose.

1810 started badly. On 14 January her mother died, and was buried beside the infant Emma at Paddington Green. Still no money came from the Earl, and Sir Robert Greville's cheques grew later and later. Emma started to move lodgings more frequently, partly to find somewhere cheaper, partly to dodge her creditors, for she was living on credit, secured only by the hope that one day either the Earl Nelson or the government would pay her what was due. That September Mr Goldsmid committed suicide and shortly before Christmas the old Duke of Queensberry died in his bed. He left a vast estate and over £1 million in cash. His Will left Emma £500 a year for life, but his lawyers said that the estate was unable to pay.

By now her situation was as ridiculous as it was pitiful. By rights, she should have had an income of £800 from Sir

William, £500 from Nelson and £500 from Queensberry, Horatia's £400 a year, plus a modest pension from the government. In fact all she received was Horatia's £400, and about half of Sir William's legacy. Instead of at least £2,000, her receivable income never topped £1,000. She had been accused of extravagance, but if her debts are totted up, it is immediately apparent that her total spendings were well within her entitlement.

The question is, why did Emma not do something more positive about it? The answer is probably her dropsy, for one of the most insidious side-effects is a profound lethargy. To stimulate herself to do anything Emma now needed a drink. She did not become a drunkard, but even a drink was well beyond her means. To buy it meant cutting out food. Nevertheless throughout this sad period of her life, Horatia was kept clean and well fed, went to good private schools, and had lessons from a series of tutors in French and Italian. Horatia now knew that Nelson was her father, but Emma never told her that she was her mother. She thought this was in the child's interest, and in doing so denied herself the emotional comfort that Horatia could have given her.

Horatia was now an active and precocious twelve-year-old, who treated Emma as little more than a blowsy governess. For her last year or so in England, Emma is hard to trace. In April 1811, a Major Gordon who had met her at a ball in Palermo was surprised to meet a shabbily dressed woman wrapped in a town shawl taking half a dozen children for a walk on Greenwich Common. It was Emma's birthday, and she was taking Horatia and her school friends on an outing, to meet some of the heroes of Trafalgar at Greenwich Hospital. Gradually her household diminished to Horatia and herself, and her possessions to a bed, some mementos such as Nelson's blood-stained uniform, and the miniature of her by Bone. Late in December 1812 her creditors found her in Fulham and she was arrested for debt. She was ordered to live within the confines of the King's Bench Prison and was allowed to take Horatia with her. The two of them took a cheap room in what was known as a sponging house at 12 Temple Place. There on payment of 4s 6d a day she was allowed outside within what were called 'the rules'. These were as follows: 'From Great Cumber Court, in the Parish of Saint George the Martyr, in the County of Surrey, along the North Side of Dirty Lane and Melancholy Walk, to Blackfriars Road, and along the Western Side of the said Road to the Obelisk, and from thence along the South West Side of the London Road, round the Direction Post in the Centre of the Roads near the Public House known by the Sign of the Elephant and Castle; from thence along the Eastern Side of Newington Causeway to Great Cumber Court aforesaid. And it is also ordered, that the New Gaol, shall be within and Part of the said Rules: And it is lastly ordered, that all Taverns, Victualling Houses, Alehouses, all Wines Vaults, and Houses or Places licensed to sell Gin or other Spirituous Liquors, shall be excluded and deemed no Part of the said Rules.'

Emma spent her time teaching Horatia French and Italian, and writing letters. She wrote to a neighbour at Merton asking them to help old Dame Francis, her former nursery maid. To another former neighbour she sold her bed and Nelson's blood-stained coat. Slowly she raised enough to buy her release, but it was short-lived. She had time to write one lengthy petition to the Price of Wales, begging him to try and use his influence to get her the moneys due to her, but hardly had it been despatched, when she was arrested again, this time on a writ for £1,000 from a carriage-maker. Sir William, apparently, had never paid for his last chariot.

This time she was to spend a year in the King's Bench. The experience would have crushed almost anyone, let alone an ailing woman with a child to look after. She was allowed to buy food if she had any money, and even her small amount of money for food dwindled when Sir Robert Greville refused to pay her the allowance Sir William had left, on the grounds that if he did, and she did not pay her creditors with it, then those same creditors might look to him. It was a petty excuse and Emma must have felt that the world had fallen in on her. Her one comfort was that she still had a few friends, and with their assistance she decided on one last determined effort. Her plan was magnificent in its insolence, its enterprise and its imagination. Early in December she wrote to the Prince of Wales, and invited him to come to take dinner with her in the debtor's prison. It was a Nelsonian tactic, and it worked. His Royal Highness accepted and asked if he might bring his current flame, a Mrs Bugge.

Emma borrowed as much cutlery and silver plate as she could. One inmate lent her a tablecloth, others glasses. The Matchams sent her a turkey, and she pawned Horatia's christening mug to buy wine. She invited an old naval friend, Sir William Dillon, to make the four. It was an extraordinary occasion, probably unique in the history of the King's Bench. Fortunately Sir William Dillon described it in his diary:

'I found a letter from Lady Hamilton inviting me to dine with her. Three years had elapsed since I had seen her . . . When the hour approached, the rain was pouring down in torrents. I engaged a postchaise for the remainder of the evening, then started for the residence indicated.

Upon my arrival her Ladyship greeted me most sincerely. "How did you know I was in town?" I demanded. She acquainted me that a friend who had seen me at the Admiralty had told her, and that she was highly delighted to shake me again by the hand. I noticed a splendid display of plate on the table, and covers laid for four, but made no enquiries who the guests were . . . While we were thus occupied, I was surprised by the entrance into the room of H.R.H. Soon afterwards Mrs Bugge made her appearance. The Prince was all kindness, and wondered I had not been to see him . . .

The dinner being served, the conversation turned in another direction. I had to do the honours—carve, etc. The first course went off on complete order, and I could not help thinking that rather too much luxury had been produced. H.R.H. did not expect such an entertainment from the lady who received him. However, there was a sad falling off in the second course, and a great deficiency in attendance, as also of knives and forks. I had to carve a good-sized bird, but had not been supplied with the necessary implements. Time passed on, but no servant made his appearance. At last Lady H. said: "Why don't you cut up that bird?" I told her I was in want of a knife and fork. "Oh!" she said, "you must not be particular here." "Very well my lady," I rejoined. "I did not like to commit myself in the presence of H.R.H. You are aware that, as a midshipman, I learnt how to use my fingers!" Then looking round, I found what I wanted, and soon had the bird in pieces. My reply produced some hearty laughter, and the repast terminated very merrily. After a sociable and agreeable entertainment, I took my leave of the company.'

The party was a success and so, it appeared, was Emma's stratagem. The Prince did start to pressure the Treasury, but then came a disaster that was as absolute as it was totally unexpected. When Emma had been arrested she had left her private papers in a suitcase with a Mr Clarke, whom she employed to draft her petitions to the Treasury. Mr Clarke was a solicitor's clerk who also earned a little extra money proof-reading for publishers. He must have read Emma's papers, which contained all Nelson's letters to her, and he must also have appreciated their value.

In the spring of 1814 two volumes entitled *The Letters of Lord Nelson to Lady Hamilton with a supplement of Interesting Letters by Distinguished Characters* were published anonymously. They were the centre of a furious scandal, for they left nothing to the imagination. His Royal Highness, who found himself described by a morbidly jealous Nelson as a 'frequenter of pimps and bawds' and sundry other equally derogatory remarks, promptly lost interest in Emma's case. He and almost everyone else believed that Emma was responsible for their publication.

By the end of June 1814 Emma's health was a grave cause for concern to the authorities and when two old friends negotiated her temporary release, she and Horatia were slipped £50 and two single tickets to Calais. They boarded the channel packet, the *Little Tom*, at Tower Bridge and are recorded as having landed in France on 3 July. A letter from Emma to Mr George Rose, an Under Secretary at the Admiralty, gives us some clues as to who was responsible for her release.

Hotel Dessin, Calais, 4 July

'We arrived here safe, dear Sir, after three days' sickness at sea, as for precaution we embarked at the Tower. Mr Smith got me the discharge from Lord Ellenborough. I then begged Mr Smith to withdraw his bail for I would have died in prison sooner than the good man should have suffered for me, and I managed so well with Horatia alone that I was at Calais before any new writs could be issued out against me. I feel so much better, from change of climate, food, air, large rooms and liberty, that there is a chance I may live to see Horatia brought up. I am looking out for lodging. I have an excellent Frenchwoman who is good at everything; for Horatia and myself, and my old dame who is coming, will be my establishment. Near me is an English lady, who has resided here for twenty-five years, who has a day school, but not for eating and sleeping. At eight in the morning, I take Horatia; fetch her at one; at three we dine, and then in the evening we walk. She learns everything—piano, harp, languages grammatically. She knows French and Italian well, but she will improve. Not any girls but those of the first families go there. Last evening we walked two miles to a *fête champêtre pour les bourgeois*. Everybody is pleased with Horatia ... If, my dear Sir, Lord Sidmouth would do something for dear Horatia, so that I can be enabled to give her an education, and also for her dress, it would ease me, for you do not know how limited I am as to money. I have left everything to be sold for the creditors, who do not deserve anything, for I have been the victim of artful mercenary wretches, and my too great liberality and open heart has been the dupe of villains. To you, Sir, I trust, for my dearest Horatia, to exert yourself for me, etc.'

The faithful Dame Francis arrived at the end of the month, and the two elderly women settled in lodgings in a little farmhouse at St Pierre, some two miles outside Calais. The sole income for the family was now Horatia's £400 a year, and much of this went on her education. Fortunately an old friend, Sir William Scott, a well known lawyer, had at last shamed Earl Nelson into paying £225 of the £3,500 arrears of income he owed Emma, though protesting that he was too poor to do it. Sir William wrote to Emma saying he was busy trying to press the Earl to provide for them, and Emma replied:

'Many thanks my dear Sir William for your kind letter. If my dear Horatia was provided for, I should die happy, and if I could only now be enabled to make her more comfortable and finish her education, oh God how I would bless them that enabled me to do it. She already reads, writes and speaks Italian, French and English, and I am teaching her German and Spanish. Music she knows, but all must yet be cultivated to perfection, and then our own language, geography, arithmetic &c. &c. she knows. We read the English, Roman and Grecian history, but it is a great fatigue to me as I have been ill eight months and am now in a state of convalescence. I must be very quiet. I have been at this farmhouse six weeks; a fine garden, common large rooms. The ladies of the house lost four and twenty thousand francs a year because their sons would not serve the Emperor. I have an ass for Horatia as she wants, now she is fourteen, exercise. I go in a cart for my health—the jaundice is leaving me, but my broken heart does not leave me. I have seen enough of grandeur not to regret it, but comfort and what would make Horatia and myself live like gentlewomen would be all I wish and to live to see her well settled in the world. We have excellent beef, mutton and veal, at five pence a pound, chickens a shilling for two, partridges five for two, a turbot for half a crown; bread very cheap, milk from the cows on the common like cream, two quarts for four sous; good Bordeaux wine tenpence a bottle. All our mornings are given up to studies.

We walk and dine at two, go in my cart, she on her donkey, everybody very kind to us. Every Wednesday there is a dance, where all the persons of rank and their daughters dance, a mile from this place, we pay threepence for going in. Horatia is adored. She dances all their dances and speaks French like a French girl. She is good, virtuous and religious. We go to the Church of St Peters and read our prayers in French for they are exactly like our own.

But, my dear Sir William, without a pound in my pocket what can I do? The 21 October, fatal day, I shall have some. I wrote to Davison to ask the Earl to let me have my Bronte pension quarterly instead of half yearly and the Earl refused, saying he was too poor—altho' I got the good and great Nelson that estate by means of the Queen. I set out from town ten weeks or more ago with not quite £50, paying our passage also out of it. Think then of the situation of Nelson's child and Lady Hamilton, who so much contributed to the Battle of the Nile, paid often and often out of my own pocket at Naples for to send to Sir John Jervis provisions, and also at Palermo for corn to save Malta. Indeed I have been ill used. Lord Sidmouth is a good man and Lord Liverpool is also an upright minister, pray do, if ever Sir William Hamilton's and Nelson's services were deserving, ask them to aid us. Think what I must feel, who was used to give God only knows too much—and now to ask. Earl and Countess Nelson lived with me, seven years I educated Lady Charlotte and paid Eton for Trafalgar's education. I made Lord Nelson write the letter to Lord Sidmouth for the prebendary at Canterbury which his Lordship kindly gave, and they have never given the dear Horatia a frock nor a sixpence. But no more for you will be tired, but my heart is full. May God bless you and yours prays, my dear Sir William, your ever grateful, Emma Hamilton.

P.S. I again before God declare I knew not of the publication of those stolen letters and I have taken the sacrament on it. Horatia begs her love.'

By Christmas her money had almost run out. Dame

Francis found cheaper lodgings in the Rue Fraglais in the poorer section of Calais, but the move taxed Emma's strength. A chill she caught brought on pneumonia, and this worsened when she went out to pawn her remaining trinkets for 225 francs. She took to her bed on 10 January, and after receiving communion died peacefully on the morning of 15 January.

Earl Nelson came over to go through her papers and with a bad grace paid Horatia's passage to England where she lived with the Machams until she married. The Earl redeemed the few items of jewellery that he fancied from the pawnshop and left in a hurry, leaving Emma's friends and neighbours from Merton to pay for her funeral. All trace of her grave has been lost, but her simplicity, her courage and her vital beauty have ensured that with all her faults it is not her enemies but Emma who has been remembered.

INDEX